WEST HIGHLAND WALKS: TWO

HAMISH MacINNES

WEST HIGHLAND WALKS: TWO
SKYE TO CAPE WRATH

'Pleasure is the outcome of exercise'
Motto of Clan MacInnes

HODDER AND STOUGHTON
LONDON SYDNEY AUCKLAND TORONTO

Acknowledgments

Photographs by Hamish MacInnes. Photographic artwork by Graeme Hunter.

British Library Cataloguing in Publication Data

MacInnes, Hamish
  West Highland Walks
  2: Skye to Cape Wrath
  1. Highlands (Scotland)—Description and travel—Guide-books
  I. Title
  914.11′804858   DA880.H7

ISBN-0-340-35972-2

Contents

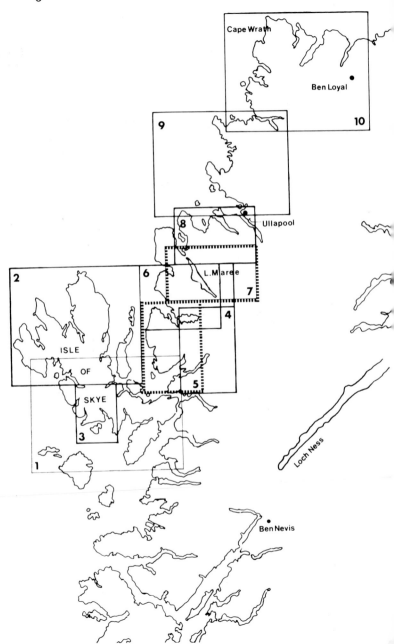

Introduction

IT HAS BEEN a longstanding ambition of mine to produce a book on the Highlands which would reflect a little of how I see this rugged, windswept land. I am indebted for the years of sheer pleasure which these lochs, mountains and moorlands have given me; their solitude and the fascination of their history. In time one begins to assemble the jigsaw complexities of clan feuds and the pattern of life which evolved from the desolate glens. Glens made increasingly desolate by the Clearances when sheep replaced families, and Highlanders who had tilled their land and tended their beasts for centuries, were themselves herded like animals, driven to the shores to make way for sheep and told to "fish or die". From 1763–75, twenty thousand people left for America alone; the majority of these were voluntary emigrants from the Highlands and Islands.

I have tried to portray with my cameras the many and varied moods of the Western Highlands, including also the places of greatest historical interest. But my attempt must inevitably fall short of the ideal and I hope that readers will feel inclined to go and see for themselves; in so doing they will be amply rewarded.

Had I shared the view of Henry Ford who said "History is bunk", I should not have written anything at all. But, out of consideration for his and similar opinions, I have kept the text concise and appreciate that many historical gaps must be spanned by the discerning reader, for whom there is fortunately a wide choice of literature.

Some people (especially the English) state that the two most consistent factors in the Scottish Highlands are the rain and the midges: true perhaps, at least for the midsummer visitor. Spring and autumn are usually the best and driest months to holiday in Scotland, spring being the most favoured season for though there may be snow on the tops in May, it complements the freshness of the glens and the sharpness of the air often gives desert-like clarity.

The area covered in this book is from Kyle of Lochalsh to Cape Wrath, including the Isle of Skye. Many of the roads in this region are single track and the country between them is the most remote and wild in Britain. The weather too can be wild and conditions are well summed up by Allan Ramsay:

> To wade through glens wi' chorking feet,
> When neither plaid nor kilt could fend the weet;
> Yet blythely wad he bang out o'er the brae,
> And stend o'er burns as light as ony rae,
> Hoping the morn might prove a better day.

To get to know Scotland, roads and cars should be left behind. Indeed I sometimes find a vehicle can be a positive hindrance in some of the more out of the way places; it is often much easier to continue on foot, than to return to a car.

Although there is no law of trespass in Scotland, and many of the old tracks are rights of way, it is better to ask permission before venturing over the hills and through the glens, especially during the stalking season which starts in September on most estates. But it is worth noting that land under the benevolent care of the National Trust for Scotland is not subject to any restrictions at such times.

In compiling this book I have attempted to cater for all degrees of energy expenditure, from the leisurely prospect of viewing a castle which entails a five minute stroll from one's car, to long and strenuous walks into remote but rewarding recesses of the Western Highlands. Where possible I have included variations to walks which will enable a change of plan should the weather deteriorate and, with a bit of judicious map study on the part of the walker, other alternatives will become apparent. Having been fortunate enough to see the region covered in this book over a period of years, in all sorts of weather, I have tried to present a balanced coverage of places of historical interest, together with walks in areas of scenic beauty. Beauty however is in the eye of the beholder and perhaps not many readers would agree with me when I say that the Rannoch Moor has a peculiar fascination in a winter's blizzard or that the naked rock of Sutherland adopts a fresh charm in rain and mist.

Included in the text are some walks for the younger at heart which include overnighting, either in a tent or in a bothy but the majority of the walks can be done in a day, or part of a day. Fortunately or unfortunately, depending on the way you look at it, some of the walks don't end at the same point as you start from. This may cause complications but I feel that this can add that bit of zest to the day's adventure and, after all, if wouldn't any longer be the wilds of Scotland if there was a shuttle service between lonely Highland glens.

As I have spent a considerable part of my career rescuing people from the hills and mountains of Scotland, I cannot stress too strongly the need for readers to take care on these moors and hills. The maps in this book show the routes of the walks described, but they are meant only for general placing reference, and walkers taking the longer hikes into secluded parts or mountainous areas should take more detailed maps with them as well. Sudden adverse weather may necessitate a change of plan, and here also a more detailed map of a wider area becomes an essential as does a compass and, still more important, the ability to use both correctly.

The West Coast presents a complicated, loch-indented coastline, rather like a frayed cloth. The hills are relatively low, but they are also exposed to the wide Atlantic: wind and storm can blow up very quickly indeed, occasionally even bringing snow to the higher tops in summer. When venturing onto the mountains be prepared with adequate clothing, a map, compass and spare food. The spring snow can linger into summer in north-facing corries and there are often frosts at this time of year. The snow surface can become very hard and correspondingly treacherous to the unwary. Therefore always choose your route according to prevailing conditions and the speed of the party. Since this book caters for such a wide age and fitness group, I have omitted any reference to time in respect of the various walks. As long as enough daylight is allowed for the return trip, without being too tired, any one of the expeditions should be safely within the capabilities of the average walker.

The central region of the West Highlands is crammed with history. In the distant past Mesolithic people, including the flint users who emigrated from Ireland to the Scottish mainland, moved northwards through this area, but left little evidence of their simple way of life. It was probably the Neolithic tribes which succeeded them who constructed the chambered cairns. They were a race of seafarers who came up the West Coast from the Mediterranean. The vitrified forts were built much later, during the Iron Age. Their pattern of distribution suggests that enemies approached from the east; the brochs too were of this period and were probably a development of the dun or fort. Brochs are only found in the north and west of Scotland; they are circular with very thick walls, sometimes up to 40ft (12m) high, through which run galleries. Typically, the only entrance was a low, narrow doorway. Brochs were possibly built as refuges against sea-raiders, or in defence against the "Fort People" from the east.

The Picts first appear in history at the tail end of the third century AD. There are records of them fighting the Romans; so persistent was their harassment that the effective influence of the Roman Empire was pushed back to the Forth-Clyde boundary; later it receded even further south to Hadrian's Wall.

Scots moved over from Ireland in increasing numbers early in the sixth century. They were a Gaelic speaking people who brought Christianity with them. In 563 Columba founded the Celtic Church which flourished for five centuries and, from his base in Iona, commenced the conversion of the Picts, travelling as far as the Pictish capital at Inverness to convert King Brude.

A great struggle ensued between the Picts and the Scots, the latter being ultimately victorious, and in 843 Kenneth MacAlpin became the first King of Scotland. With the passage of time, and partly due to the influence of David I (1124–53), a division again became apparent in Scotland. He introduced feudalism by making grants of land, especially up the eastern coastal plain and along the Moray Firth. The Celtic, Gaelic speaking people of the north and west bitterly opposed this Anglicisation, with the result that the geographical boundaries of the Highland Celt commenced with the mountains and embraced the Highland regions of Scotland. Here they developed as a separate people with their own language and culture, living under a totally different structure of society: the clan system. It was a family union, where the members were united under a chief, and each member of the tribe or clan bore the same name.

The Norsemen came in a series of invasions and dominated the western seaboard for four centuries but by the mid-thirteenth century the Scots had overrun the Viking colony of north Scotland and had occupied the Hebrides. The Vikings were finally defeated at the Battle of Largs in 1263, but they have left their mark in the place-names and culture of the Highlands.

The centuries following were times of anarchy. The Western Highlands were little influenced by the wars to the south – even the War of Independence in which starred the indomitable Bruce. But it was an era of bloody deeds in the lawless Highlands: of repeated massacres and reprisals. A verse which holds more than a grain of truth tells that after God made the Highlander from horse droppings:

> Quoth God to the Highlander, "What will you now?"
> "I will go to the Lowland, Lord, and there steal a
> cow . . ."

After the fall of the Stewarts and the upsurge of Jacobitism, the Highlands again became ensnared in the web of Scottish politics. Clans had merged for mutual protection, giving birth to such powerful confederations as that of the MacDonalds under one supreme chief who, from about 1354, took the title of the Lord of the Isles.

Both James III and James IV did much to subjugate the unruly clansmen. Between 1493 and 1499 James IV sailed to Western Scotland six times and many Highlanders fought for him at Flodden; he had a smattering of the Gaelic which enhanced his popularity with the clansmen. The Campbells under the Earls and later the Dukes of Argyll always associated themselves with the Protestant Lowlands; inevitably, they became a hated and feared clan.

Despite the troubles, an oral culture survived and even prospered. Each chief had his bard who recorded events in song with verse. The bagpipe became the versatile instrument of both war and peace. During the seventeenth century and the early part of the eighteenth, the Highland scene was relatively peaceful and, during this period lived some of the greatest poets: Duncan Ban MacIntyre, Alexander Macdonald, and Rob Donn.

From time to time there were abortive attempts to win back the throne for the Stewarts, but the one with the most far-reaching effects proved to be the Jacobite rising of 1745 which changed the course of Highland history, bequeathing an aftermath of misery and depredation. It now seems incredible that the adventurer, Prince Charles Edward, could have rallied the clans as he did, arriving from France without money or arms, with a surplus only of confidence. What the young Prince lacked in pistols and louis d'or, he made up for in eloquence and personality. One is forced to admire his audacity and regret his final decline in exiled defeat: he eventually died an alcoholic. Prince Charlie's trail whilst fleeing from Cumberland's troops after his defeat at Culloden, zig-zags through the following pages like an historical meteor.

The punitive measures employed against the Highlanders after the 'Forty-five were crushing indeed. Men loyal to the Crown fared little better than those with Jacobite sympathies. Wearing of Highland dress was prohibited and the penalty for simply playing the pipes could be transportation. The chiefs were deprived of all authority over their clans, whilst the Disarming Act forbade the carrying of weapons by the clansmen. Gaelic speech, too, was discouraged. These acts above all caused the disintegration of the clans. Some of the laws were not rescinded for thirty years; others not at all.

The chiefs became lairds. There was a boom in cattle, so many of the chiefs either sold or leased their land to the highest bidder. The old way of life was totally disrupted and emigration increased. Then a series of famines occurred between 1768 and 1773: crops failed and the cattle died. The destitute people clothed only in sacking scoured the beaches for edible shellfish.

Later the cattle trade declined and, in the late eighteenth century, it was realised that sheep were able to weather the Highland winter and provide an alternative. This discovery marked the beginning of the Clearances; people were thrown out of their houses, many of which were subsequently burned, and forced to move to the coast or emigrate. The sheep needed space. . . On one occasion a shipload of Camerons arrived in Sydney and a man, scanning the passenger list, was heard to exclaim, "Look here, the Camerons will soon be filling the country. Over two hundred of them have arrived on this one ship!"

People often wonder why the Highlanders accepted the Clearances so humbly – there was very little bloodshed. This was mainly due to the fact that the menfolk were away fighting in the Napoleonic Wars and the clergy, who wielded a powerful influence over the people, ignobly supported the lairds. But the Clearances were economically inevitable.

The decline in the Highlander's traditional way of life had a drastic effect on his outlook. The most enterprising travelled overseas; those who stayed were not helped by the rigid discipline of religion and suffered severe hardships. The numerous men who were evicted to the coast built hovels, fished and tried to raise crops without any security of tenure. They were at the mercy of the factors and the landowners, with no legal redress since the lairds were also the magistrates. At this time, in the late nineteenth century, dissatisfaction was growing. . . Deer forests and grouse moors had become fashionable for the rich and in some areas crofters were forbidden to repair leaking roofs with rushes or heather because the removal of the raw material might cause the grouse discomfort! Crops were eaten and trampled by marauding deer; but deer, to the common crofter, were untouchable.

The tinder was set alight at Braes in Skye when irate women forced police to burn an eviction notice. But the law returned, spurred on by an enraged Inverness magistrate. Sixty police under two sheriffs and officers arrived at Braes, close to Portree. The Battle of the Braes was fought with batons and stones. No lives were lost but a battered police posse limped back to Portree. Gladstone, who was Prime Minister at the time, was concerned. Warships were sent to the island and troops landed, but the population of Braes was unimpressed. Following this incident the Government at last realised the injustices which the Highlanders were enduring; the result was the Crofters Holding Act, 1886, which gave the crofters security of tenure. Nowadays the croft is too small a unit to be commercially viable and crofters usually hold another job as well. Inevitably the young people move into the cities, seeking work, and the proportion of the elderly increases each year in crofting communities.

The discovery of oil has for the present given a fresh lease of life to the Highlands, and several new industries have been created; some, alas, accompanied by pollution. It is time people realised that Scotland's greatest heritage lies in its unspoiled scenery: seemingly unproductive, wild tracts of country are its most valuable asset. Over the years the Highlands have scarcely altered; Glen Sligachan is probably the same now as when a tired Prince Charlie squelched through its bogs in 1746. Let us hope that in the future this unique land will not be exploited beyond retrieval, but allowed to remain essentially a "Wilderness" area within our nation.

Skye, Isle of Mists

ANT-EILEAN SGIATHANACH is what the Gaels called Skye; it means the Winged Isle. This name seems appropriate enough, for its many peninsulas reach far out into the sea. The Norsemen called it the Cloud Island, Skuyo, which description the regular visitor to the Cuillin may well appreciate. Norsemen occupied the island for three centuries and left behind a legacy of place names – Vaternish, Troddhay, Harbost – which are still in common use. The two ancient clans of the island are the MacDonalds and the MacLeods. Skye, including the adjoining islands of Raasay and Scalpay, covers 650 square miles. Its population in 1841 was 23,074, and in 1971, 7,481.

Road and railway both meet and end at Kyle of Lochalsh on the Scottish mainland; across the channel between Kyle and Kyleakin there is a ferry. In 1263 the ageing King Haco took his longships through these narrows and anchored at Sgeir na Cailliche, the Carlon Stone, to the north of the entrance of Kyle Rhea. On the shore at Kyleakin are the ruins of an old fort, Casteal Maol. A Norse princess is reputed to have exacted a toll on ships using the straits by spanning the channel with a chain. Alternative ways of reaching the Isle of Mist are by 'plane to Broadford, or by ferry from Mallaig to Armadale, or Glenelg to Kylerhea.

Between Kyleakin and Kylerhea are the much neglected hills, Beinn na Caillich (2,396ft/730m) and Sgurr na Coinnich (2,424ft/739m). Both these mountains offer eagle's eye views of the narrows of Kyle Rhea and the sweeping tide race. Cattle used to be swum across here during the great droving days, when it used to take the drovers twenty-eight days to travel from Dunvegan on Skye to the Falkirk or Crieff trysts. (In 1723 30,000 black cattle were driven to Crieff market and sold for 30,000 guineas.) One old drover I spoke to,

Casteal Maol, Kyleakin, Skye, with the mainland behind. ▶

used to return to Skye by steamer from Glasgow but his six dogs had to find their own way back and would sometimes be home before him.

Skye is an island of forts and virtually every headland commanding a prominent situation was capped by a dun at one time. There are few trees on the island, other than those in Sleat, and the new plantations being developed by the Forestry Commission which cover about 5,000 acres. The two main ranges of hills in Skye are the Black Cuillin and the Red Cuillin. The Black Cuillin curve round the enclosed waters of Loch Coruisk in the shape of a gigantic horseshoe, thereby forming the narrowest ridge in the British Isles; but to the east the granite peaks of the Red Cuillin are more gentle, some carpeted in grass almost to their summit; others capped by scree. In the north of the island beyond Portree, the largest town, are the hills of Storr. Yet further north again in this most northerly wing of the island, are the contorted pinnacles of the Quirang, looking like a gallery of witches.

Sleat, Broadford and Blaven

SLEAT – "THE LEVEL Land" – is the southernmost peninsula in Skye. It is probably flatter than the other wings of the island and it certainly possesses more natural forest which gives the region a more intimate appearance than the starker areas to the north and west. Past Isleornsay, a small, sleepy village boasting a lighthouse and superb outlook across the Sound of Sleat to Knoydart, a road cuts across the spine of the peninsula.

◄ *Isleornsay, the Sound of Sleat, with the mainland peaks beyond.*

Blaven and Clach Glas, from near Ord, Sleat. ►

Tarskavaig, the west coast of Sleat. In the background Glen Sligachan divides the Main Black Cuillin range on the left and Blaven, right. ► ►

Before reaching Ord on the west coastline of Sleat, one passes the remains of a small wood, Coille a' Ghasgain. In ancient times this was a sanctuary. Anyone was safe here, no matter what crime he had committed. At Ord itself there are the ruins of an old church, Teampuill Chaon, which is dedicated to St. Comgan, patron saint of Lochalsh. Ancient graves lie close to the church but nothing is known of their history today.

The western aspect of Sleat is possibly the most scenic in Skye, with magnificent views across Lochs Eishort and Slapin on a good day, to the gabbro upthrusts of the Black Cuillin with Blaven and Clach Glas. Small bays and beaches nudge this coastline; stunted oaks, ash and hazel struggle against the wrath of Atlantic storms. At one time the old fort of Dun Sgathaich, on the shore a little way south of Ord, was of great importance. It perches in ruined splendour on a rocky tooth, separated from the headland by a shallow moat. An arched bridge, now unsafe, still remains. The dun can be reached by crossing the moat and scrambling up the side nearest the road. The MacAskills were its custodians for the Norse kings of Man, but Dun Sgathaich's history reaches right back into the dimmest past, as it was the fort of Scathach, a warrior queen whose most famous pupil was Cuchulainn, the Irish warrior. Tradition relates that Dun Sgathaich was built by fairies in a single night. One can only regret that they do not indulge in construction works more often!

There was a gruesome plot within the family of the first chief of Sleat. Donald Herrach, the third son, owned lands in Uist. His illegitimate brother, Gillespic Dubh, was determined to obtain some of (as he believed) his rightful possessions, so he paid a visit to his brother in Uist. As was the custom in those days, the

---

◄ *Dun Sgathaich (pronounced Skaich) on the west coast of Sleat, once a very important stronghold. The Red Cuillin in the background.*

men indulged in feats of strength and athletics. Gillespic suggested an unusual competition: to touch a noose of rope hanging from a beam with the chin. The other end of the rope was held by Gillespic's accomplice, Pol na h-eile (Paul of the Thong). Donald was by far the fittest and, as was anticipated, jumped the highest. Once his neck was firmly in the noose and he was dangling helplessly, red hot irons were thrust into his bowels to finish off the job. Gillespic hot-footed it back to Dun Sgathaich where his other brother, the chief, was constructing a new galley. Proudly the chief showed Gillespic over the vessel but, as he bent down during the inspection, his brother stabbed him with a dirk; the chief died shortly afterwards. Gillespic's stay in Sleat was short-lived, however, for he was chased out of the area and took up a life of piracy. Later he betrayed his compatriots and received a Royal Pardon. He was finally killed by Ronald Herrach, a nephew, who later paid a visit to a crowded Dun Sgathaich. On this visit Ronald was taken aback at the conduct of some of the Clan Ranald in his ancestral home. That night he killed twelve of them and hung them from the walls in view of the bedroom of Catherine of Clan Ranald, wife of the chief, who was also staying there. The incensed Catherine hired an assassin who eventually found Ronald in Griminish, in North Uist, and murdered him.

In 1431 an insurrection against the Government instigated by Donald Balloch, was vigorously suppressed by King James I who took Sleat and the castles of Camus and Dun Sgathaich. Later, too, after the battle of Flodden, a new insurrection began and the MacLeod chief was one of the prime movers. The rebel chiefs held a meeting at Casteal Maol in 1513 and Sir Donald MacDonald of Lochalsh was created Lord of the Isles.

◄ *Camus Castle and Knock Bay. On the shore, close to the castle, a naval party was hanged from gibbets made from oars.*

Dun Sgathaich was stormed and badly damaged before it was taken by Alasdair Crotach of Dunvegan on behalf of the Lord of the Isles; but a siege on Camus Castle at Knock was to no avail, despite protracted efforts. The successful defence was conducted, it is said, by one Mary of the Castle!

In summer, driving on Skye can have its problems. Once off the main highway, however, one gets the impression that the byways, when not caravan consti-pated, are still much as they were when Prince Charlie traversed them, with the dubious advantage of a cursory coating of instant tar which melts at the first hint of summer. But when Camus Castle was built at Knock Bay, four miles north-east of Armadale, the sea was the highway. Not much remains of Camus Castle now; it has been strangled by ivy. From the road one can look across the small bay to the ruins set on a rocky mound. It belonged originally to the MacLeods. In 1690 William of Orange dispatched two warships into the Sound of Sleat to arrest Sir Donald MacDonald and they landed a party at Armadale which razed the chief's house to the ground. They were captured, however, and hanged at the castle beach from gibbets constructed out of their own oars.

The present Armadale Castle is set deep in the woods, close to the main road. The building is rela-tively modern, being built in 1815 as the seat of Lord MacDonald. Now, due to a disastrous fire, only a shell remains but the woods are well worth a visit and are open to the public.

From Armadale a ferry crosses to Mallaig whilst the

◄ *Armadale Castle, Sleat, Skye.*

Broadford from the main Kyleakin – Portree road. Beinn ►
na Caillich, behind the village, gives an easy climb.
Beneath the summit cairn a Norse princess is buried.

The peaks of the Blaven group from Loch Slapin. There ► ►
are three corries on the east face.

road continues south to the village of Ardvasar where a track leads on to the Point of Sleat with its many sandy bays facing Arisaig, Eigg and Rhum.

Travelling north again, Broadford is a wet place, the annual rainfall of eighty-seven inches, influenced no doubt by the Cuillin. From here a road cuts across to Loch Slapin and on to Elgol. Just after leaving the village, the ruins of Coire Chatachan are seen to the right on the lower slopes of Beinn na Caillich (not to be confused with the hill between Kyleakin and Kylerhea). It was here that Boswell and Johnson were entertained on two occasions by the MacKinnons. Though Dr Johnson soon retired to bed, Boswell partook of some punch, then some more and, as he later confessed, they were "cordial and merry to a high degree. Of what passed I have no recollection with any accuracy . . ." Next day, about one o'clock, Johnson went to Boswell's room and remarked in a jocular fashion, "What, drunk yet?"

As in life, so in death. When Sir Alexander MacDonald died in the barracks at Glenelg in 1746, he was carried to Kilmore in Sleat for burial. The event was long remembered for the incredible wake which accompanied it. The enormous sum (in those days) of £2,645 was spent, mainly on drink. Inevitably at such a party fights took place. "Three men were killed and fifty taken out of the churchyard with the breath just left in them." It is also recorded that wheelbarrows were used for carrying off the unconscious.

Blaven means the Hill of Bloom; seen from Torrin, with the fields and Loch Slapin as foreground, it is difficult to imagine a more perfect setting. The traverse of the ridge of Blaven and Clach Glas is an expedition for mountaineers only, due to complex route finding, but Blaven itself offers no great difficulty if approached

▲ ◄ *On Loch Scavaig, Loch Coruisk is in the hollow slightly right of centre. The Bad Step is on the rocky right-hand shore.*

◄ *Loch Coruisk from above Loch Scavaig.*

with care. Follow the Allt na Dunaiche stream, to the right of the house in the picture on page 31, and take the left-hand stream at the junction which leads into Fionna Choire. Ascend steeply to the ridge, left in the picture, and follow the easiest line to the summit. An alternative approach is by the long easy ridge running up from Camasunary at the south end of Glen Sligachan. Needless to say, the ascent should not be attempted under mist. The summit of Blaven's northern top overlooks the sweep of Glen Sligachan, a great corridor flanked by some of the mightiest mountains in Skye. From here too, on a good day, the full range of the Black Cuillin can be seen. It is possibly the best vantage point on the whole island. From the summit of Blaven, Loch Coruisk appears secreted within a deep defile in the heart of the range; the easiest way to visit it is to take a boat to the head of Loch Scavaig and then walk the short distance to its rugged shores.

An alternative route to Coruisk follows a track westward from the road, just past Kilmarie; it is well signposted and cuts across the back of Strathaird peninsula where the Cuillin appear to the north-west in a dramatic and savage attitude. The cottage of Camasunary is reached at the mouth of Glen Sligachan. Having crossed the river, the track skirts round Sgurr na Stri to the rock-studded inner bay of Loch Scavaig. Here is the Bad Step which can easily be negotiated about fifteen feet above high water mark. From the head of the small bay, a brief walk across a rocky neck of

---

◄ *The Great Prow in the middle corrie on the east side of Blaven.*

The Bad Step with Loch Scavaig behind. ►

From near the summit of the north peak of Blaven, looking up Glen Sligachan to Sgurr nan Gillean (peak touching clouds). Harta Corrie is seen on the left, branching off Glen Sligachan, beyond the loch. ► ►

land leads straight to Loch Coruisk. Sir Walter Scott wrote of his visit, "We lost sight of the sea almost immediately after we had climbed over a low ridge of crags, and were surrounded by mountains of naked rock, of the boldest and most precipitous character. The ground on which we walked was the margin of a lake, which seemed to have sustained the constant ravage of torrents from these rude neighbours." Coruisk, or Coir' Uisg, to give it its Gaelic name, means Corrie of Water: well-named indeed.

As suggested, the easiest way of reaching the loch is to go by sea from Elgol; during the summer months there are several boats each day. It was from Elgol that Prince Charlie sailed to Mallaigvaig in July 1745 with MacKinnon, the aged chief, when he left Skye for the last time.

The Isle of Raasay and Roderick the Venomous

FOLLOWING THE COAST road north-west from Broadford, the Red Hills stand on the left, stately in their own way, offering limited grazing only to the black-faced sheep and the occasional deer. Both the Red Hills and the Black Cuillin are composed of igneous rock, but the Red Hills present blunt granite summits to the heavens, in contrast to their stark neighbours formed from dark gabbro.

Just past Sconser Lodge Hotel, at the entrance to Loch Sligachan, is the Raasay ferry pier; a good view of the island, dominated by its highest hill, Dun Caan, is obtained from here. The narrow channel of the Atlantic between Skye and Raasay contains the deepest water in the British coastal seas, with fissures of over 1,500ft gouged out by the Loch Alsh glacier.

◀ *The Cuillin from Elgol.*

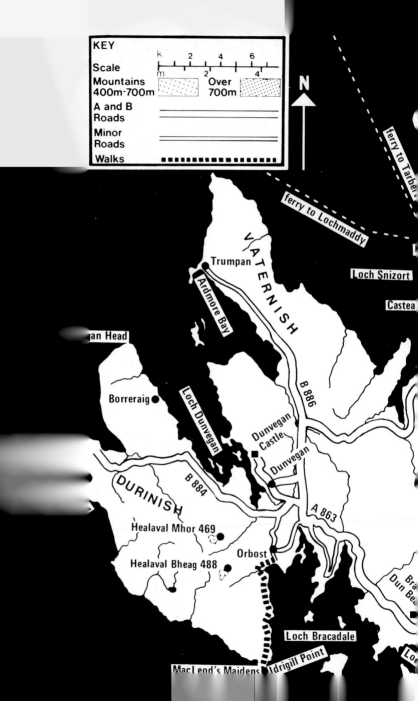

KEY

Scale

Mountains 400m-700m | Over 700m

A and B Roads

Minor Roads

Walks

N

ferry to Tarbert

ferry to Lochmaddy

Loch Snizort

Castea

VATERNISH

Trumpan

Ardmore Bay

an Head

Borreraig

Loch Dunvegan

B 886

Dunvegan Castle

Dunvegan

DURINISH

B 884

A 863

Healaval Mhor 469

Healaval Bheag 488

Orbost

Bra Dun Bea

Loch Bracadale

MacLeod's Maidens Idrigill Point

Lo

On the east side of Raasay lie the ruins of Brochel Castle which, according to tradition, was built by the MacSwans who occupied the island before the MacLeods. In the year 1539 John of the Axe (Iain na Tuaighe) had an affair with the wife of his uncle, Roderick MacLeod, tenth Baron of Lewis. She came to live with him on Raasay but the fact that she was a MacKenzie, with whom the Raasay clan were at war, did not endear her to the locals. John of the Axe was guardian to the heir of the second chief of Raasay, and after his first wife died he married a kinswoman, possibly to placate his clansmen. In so doing he acquired a brother-in-law who rejoiced in the name of Roderick the Venomous (Nimheach) who was notorious, even in those days of dark dealings and murder. Upon the birth of a son to the second marriage of John with his sister, Roderick conceived a plot to further his own ends, and dispatched urgent messages to Raasay, inviting John and all the kinsmen of the dead chief to meet him on the Isle of Isay in Dunvegan Loch. Upon their arrival he entertained them sumptuously with generous quantities of wine, before announcing that he would first hold individual consultations with each of his relatives in turn; then, in true democratic fashion, he would later conduct an open meeting back in the banqueting hall. Upon entering the discussion chamber first, John of the Axe was dispatched by two assassins, followed shortly by the heir to the chieftainship; the remainder of the guests were eliminated in a similar fashion with the exception of his nephew. However, Roderick the Venomous had failed to dispose of the entire family; the youngest son of the previous chief survived because he had not accepted the summons. When news of the murders reached Raasay

The Island of Raasay.
An old croft house. ►
Peinchorran from across Loch Sligachan with the hills of ► ►
Storr in the distance.

he was removed and sent for safe-keeping with Campbell of Calder. Roderick took over Brochel Castle but later a band of resolute Raasay MacLeods won it back on behalf of the rightful heir. The castle was taken at night but Roderick escaped and made his way across the Inner Sound of Raasay.

The Island suffered heavily after the 'Forty-five. There were one hundred and twenty families living there when the ruthless Captain Fergusson of the *Furnace* invaded the island and laid it waste. Crops were destroyed and houses burnt; the devastation was thorough and complete. Raasay House was also destroyed by the King's orders but later a new house was built on the earlier site. There was a sanctuary and chapel beside the house; the perimeter of the sanctuary is said to have been marked by eight crosses.

More modern weapons of war are being used now in the area. Part of the Sound is used for a torpedo testing range, though little of this is visible from the island.

Sligachan has had a long association with mountaineering and many of the early routes in the Cuillin were pioneered from here. Now the nucleus of climbing has shifted to Glen Brittle, as this centre provides better access to the main rock climbing areas. The hotel (there is nothing else at Sligachan) is strategically placed at the division of the two main roads; there is excellent trout and salmon fishing.

The Battle of Sligachan between the MacLeods and the MacDonalds was fought in 1395. William Cleireach was the fourth chief of the MacLeods and had succeeded to the title upon his brother's death. Although he was educated for a life of celibacy in the church, he proved to be a great warrior and, for one boasting of such pious beginnings, sired a vast number of illegitimate children. The MacDonalds sent a powerful force in galleys to invade Skye; they successfully evaded MacAskill, Constable of Dun Sgathaich and of Rubh' an Dunain (the dun at the entrance to Loch Brittle) and landed at Eynort, creating a wave of destruction as they moved towards Sligachan. Here they met a formidable force of MacLeods and a gripping battle commenced, which ended in a rout for the MacDonalds. The MacLeods followed close on their heels as far as Loch Eynort, where the MacAskills meanwhile had taken possession of the MacDonald galleys and had moored them well off-shore. Few MacDonalds survived the ensuing carnage; the heads of the slain were gathered, numbered and forwarded to Dunvegan as trophies. The Bloody Stone in Harta Corrie, Creag an Fheannaidh (Rock of the Flaying) is reputed to be the place where the spoils of the battle were divided.

North to Trotternish: Portree, the Storr, the Quirang and a cauldron of heads

PORTREE IS THE biggest town on the island and Highland Games are held here each autumn. The name may come from the Gaelic Port an Righ (the King's harbour) or possibly from the word for forearm, *ruigh*, which is common in place names referring to ground sloping up to a hill. The bay was known as Loch Chaluimcille until James V visited it in 1540 whilst attempting to bring the Western Highlands to heel. It was in Portree also, in what is now the Royal Hotel, that Prince Charlie bade Flora MacDonald adieu.

The prominent hill to the north of Portree on the Trotternish coast is the Storr (2,358ft/719m), meaning either a rotten tooth or a large cliff. Its cliffs indeed rise 600 feet. The Old Man of Storr is the light grey basalt pinnacle, conspicuous from both road and sea. Its precarious 160 feet have been climbed and classified as Very Severe. The path up to the Old Man starts at the Forestry Commission car park. Even for the elderly, it is worth the effort to make the gradual 900 foot ascent to this natural sanctuary with its backdrop, the peaks of

Quinag and Foinaven, mystic mountains, in the far distance. All round the Old Man stand its concubines, lesser towers in various shapes and forms, all looking equally unstable. One might well name them the Tottering Towers of Trotternish. It is no area for the rock climber, the friable rock being highly dangerous, but the basaltic soil of the Storr fosters a galaxy of flowering plants, including the tiny and extremely rare *Koenigia islandica*.

The Storr can be ascended from the Snizort road, starting at the River Haultin, then following its tributary, the Lon Mor. The slopes above lead to the summit. The backbone of Trotternish may then be followed north along the escarpment; although there is no path north of the Storr, it is quite possible to carry on northwards, past Beinn Edra and gain the Uig – Staffin road. This gives a long and varied walk (16 miles) along one of the greatest cliff edges in Britain.

Loch Leathan – now harnessed for hydro-electric power – is the loch from which Young Raasay, intent on helping Prince Charlie evade Cumberland's soldiers, dragged a cockleshell of a boat down the steep slope, where the pipelines now run, to the shore at Bearreraig Bay. He didn't consider the "sieve" fit for a royal cargo so made his way gingerly over to Raasay where he quickly procured a better craft (only two had escaped the axes of Captain Fergusson's landing party which devastated the island). During the wee hours of Tuesday, July 1st, they rowed the boat over to Sgeir Mhor, close to Portree, and there collected the Prince and took him back to Raasay where they lived for a short time in a shepherd's sheiling, so low that they could hardly sit upright in it.

◄ *The route up to the Old Man of Storr takes (approx.) the right-hand skyline, from the Forestry Commission car park.*
Portree harbour.　　　　　　　　　　　　　　　　　▶
Portree and the Old Man of Storr behind.　　　　　▶ ▶

To the north of the Storr, the coast is bleak; one is conscious of the lack of trees and the cultivated land is terminated by the eastern margin of high cliffs which drop abruptly to the shore. There are ruins of duns on several promontories. At Loch Mealt, the bastion of Kilt Rock with its basaltic columns can be seen from the edge of the cliff.

Rising behind the village of Staffin is the Quirang (in Gaelic: Cuithreang – the Pillared Cattle Pen). The Trotternish landslip area stretches from the Quirang down to the Storr. The movement and collapse of the over-riding basaltic lavas on Jurassic sediments, still continuing today, has been responsible for the impressive scarp, the characteristic rugged blocks and weathered pinnacles. The Quirang can be reached most easily from the high point on the Staffin to Uig road by following a long traverse line up between the outcrop of the Prison on the right and the main mass – with the Needle conspicuous above the scree – on the left. Beyond the Needle, the Table is a flat, grassy eminence contained within the natural arena.

Little remains of the former glory of Duntulm. The castle occupies a prominent rock in the north-west corner of Skye. It was built on the site of a much older fort, Dun Dabhaid, one time home of a Norse princess called Biornal. The castle changed hands on many occasions, occupied sometimes by the Lords of the Isle and, at others, by the vassals of the Earls of Ross; but for a great part of the time it was in the possession of the MacLeods of Dunvegan. According to reports, it was a

◄ *The Old Man of Storr and his minions from the Sanctuary.*

Sea cliffs to the north of Storr. Note the lazybeds in the foreground. ►

Kilt Rock, south of Staffin, Skye, is part of a large ► ► *intrusive sill with conspicuous vertical "pleats" of basaltic columns. These have been created by contraction-fractures as the molten rock cooled.*

building of some consequence and great pains were taken with the surrounding ground, soil being brought from seven different kingdoms – Germany, Denmark, Ireland, Norway, France, Spain and England – to enrich it. A hollow hewn from the rock below the castle marks where the MacDonalds secured their galleys, and at low tide a groove is still visible in the rock down which the galleys were launched.

It was from Duntulm that Donald Gorm set off to besiege Eilean Donnan Castle, where he was wounded by the last arrow left in the castle, according to legend. His impetuosity in wrenching the arrow out of his thigh caused an artery to be severed and so he bled to death. Like many a Highland chief in those days, Donald Gorm was partial to wine. Even after his death, when his ghost returned to haunt Duntulm castle, he was accompanied by various rowdy "spiritual" friends, all apparently in an inebriated state! These spirits were partly exorcised by a nephew who, upon the advice of a saintly man, recommended that seven stout men should enter the haunted castle with lighted tapers of pine, and drive out the supernatural revellers. Tradition relates that the haunting was somewhat diminished thereafter, but the family had to abandon the castle eventually in 1539. James V was most impressed by Duntulm when he visited with his fleet in 1540.

The old dungeon of Duntulm is now filled in and in it are buried many gory tales. One relates to the death of Uisdein Mac Gillespic Chleirich (Hugh, son of Gillespic the Writer), who was obviously an opportunist without regard for human life. Whilst completing

_____

◀ *The Needle, Quirang.*

A culvert's eyeview of the Quirang. The approach is from ▶
the road, back through the defile below the main crags, or
from the high point on the road.

From the Table in the Quirang looking out over Staffin. ▶ ▶
The Needle is seen on the right of centre.

his own castle, Casteal Uisdein, a couple of miles south of Uig Bay on an outcrop of rock above the shore at South Guideach, he wrote two letters: one to the chief of Duntulm, inviting him to a house party, and the second to a hired assassin called Martin. Somehow – and it happens even today – the letters were muddled and delivered to the wrong persons.

The chief promptly took action and sent a famous swordsman to apprehend Hugh, but the wily Hugh evaded him and set sail in his galley, *An Ealadh* (the Swan), for the Outer Isles. He was followed and captured after being besieged in a small castle on an inland loch, then taken back to Duntulm where he was thrown into the dungeon. By this time, not having eaten since his capture, he was suitably famished for the chief's unique revenge, and a large portion of salted meat was placed before him; when he cried out for water an empty jug was lowered to him. Hugh was a very big man indeed; until 1827 his bones and skull were on view outside Kilmuir Church and were famed for their size.

A mile and a half south of Duntulm stand the crofts of Kilmuir and there is also a small museum with several exhibits of interest. Here is the graveyard where Flora MacDonald is buried; it was estimated that over 3,000 people attended the funeral.

The most romantic episode of all the Young Pretender's escapades was enacted in this northern part of Skye and the nearby Minch. He had fled with Flora from Rossinish in Benbecula, posing as her maid Betty Burke (a name probably borrowed from one of the Prince's stalwart friends, Edward Burke). Flora had obtained passports for their voyage to Skye, but the

◀ *Hugh's Castle, Casteal Uisdein, the unfinished fortress.*

Duntulm Castle, which is built on the site of an old Norse ▶
fort.

Flora MacDonald's monument, Kilmuir. ▶ ▶

Outer Isles were alive with troops and naval ships were everywhere. After some adventures they arrived safely at the point, Allt a' Chuain, near Kilmuir. Flora went by herself to Monkstadt House, the home of Sir Alexander and Lady Margaret MacDonald, where she had frequently stayed. It was fortunate that the Prince remained in hiding close to the shore since there were soldiers surrounding the house and officers within; one of these was General Campbell. Flora stayed for a meal with the MacDonalds and was quizzed about her voyage from the Outer Isles. Secretly, she informed her hostess that the Prince was waiting on the coast and that good lady at once sent her factor, MacDonald of Kingsburgh, with food for the Prince. Later that day, still wearing his Betty Burke disguise, the Prince walked with the factor to the latter's house. Since they were days of decorum (if not of law-abidance), MacDonald found it necessary to reprimand the Prince for lifting his skirt too high when crossing a stream. Charles also forgot himself when meeting people on the way, giving his customary bow instead of a curtsy! Others commented on the height of the "huzzy" and of the long, mannish strides she took.

Flora joined them later that night for dinner at Kingsburgh's house. After she and the factor's wife had retired, the Prince took out his pipe, "the cutty" (he suffered at the time from toothache which the tobacco smoke partially alleviated) and he and his host drank some punch. Inevitably they had more punch and eventually the prudent Kingsburgh called a halt and tried to remove the bowl; Prince Charlie resisted and grasped the bowl which was broken in the ensuing struggle and, the issue mutually settled, the Prince went to bed. Next day he continued on his peregrinations with the good Kingsburgh, once more reverting to male Highland garb.

Outer Isles ferries operate from Uig and a good road leads south and east to Portree. A pleasant excursion can be made up Glen Uig by driving up the south side of the River Conon past the volcanic pinnacles to Balnaknock. From the end of the road Corrie Amadal can be ascended and the Bealach Amadal reached on the backbone of Trotternish.

Beyond the head of Loch Snizort Beag the road branches, the right-hand fork leading back along the other shore of the loch to Edinbain and Dunvegan.

The ford at the River Snizort was the scene of great carnage in 1528: the MacDonalds and MacLeods were at it again. This time the MacLeod lands of Trotternish had been invaded and pillaged and the MacLeods driven off like cattle. The main body of those who escaped reached the ford at the mouth of the River Snizort and there resolved to make a stand. It was a bloody scene. Though the MacDonalds lost many in their crossing of the flooded river, attacked by the desperate MacLeods, they succeeded in gaining the far shore by sheer force of numbers, so that only a much depleted band of MacLeods continued their flight. So savage was the fighting that the place was afterwards known as Achadh na fala (Field of Blood). The heads of the slain combatants were gathered in a pool close to the mouth of the river, which acquired the name, Coire nan Ceann (Cauldron of Heads). The MacLeods appealed to the Government for compensation for losses incurred during the raid. The Lords of Council agreed that this should be made, but there is no record of the MacDonalds ever paying for the 800 cattle, 340 horses, 2,900 sheep and 3,100 goats which were removed.

Vaternish: the Fairy Flag and the three funerals of Lady Grange

VATERNISH IS YET another wing of Skye, pointing towards faraway Greenland. MacDonald raiders from Uist

came across the Little Minch to Vaternish in May 1578. It is said they came to revenge the Massacre of Eigg but this excuse is by no means definite fact. It was on a Sunday morning that eight galleys put into Ardmore Bay under a blanket of fog. After beaching their craft, they stole quietly up the hillside to Trumpan Church within which most of the populace was worshipping. Some stood guard at the door, making escape impossible, whilst others fired the thatch. As the congregation was mercilessly cremated, the MacDonald piper struck up a stirring tune. It is said that only one person escaped: a woman who darted past the clansmen at the door but, in so doing, had one of her breasts cut clean off by a MacDonald claymore. She died on her way home at a place which was known as Sloc Mhairearaid (the Hollow of Margaret). The communion cup which was being used in the church at the time is now in the museum at Kilmuir.

True to tradition, the pillaging MacDonalds were engaged in gathering their spoils of sheep and cattle when the MacLeods of Dunvegan swept in with their birlinns, spurred by a following wind blowing out of Loch Dunvegan. With them they carried one of the earliest secret weapons, the Bratach Sith or Fairy Flag, which had been taken out of its iron chest for this emergency. Not only does it ensure victory for the MacLeods in battle but, when hoisted at Dunvegan Castle, brings herring into the loch and also guarantees offspring, if spread on the MacLeod marriage bed. The Bratach Sith is believed to be a consecrated banner of the Knights Templar, captured from the Saracens during the Crusades. The MacLeod tradition is that it was given to the fourth chief, William, by his fairy lover on condition that it should be displayed only during three types of emergency: if the sole heir was in danger of death; if the clan was being defeated; or if the clan faced extinction. To date it

In Glen Uig, North Skye.

had been unfurled only twice in battle; each time the MacLeods were victorious. On this occasion according to a contemporary bard: "Grass blades were changed to armed men as soon as the folds of the magic banner were unfurled." Whether put to flight by the sight of the Fairy Flag, the extra "men of grass", or the angry MacLeods, the MacDonalds certainly retreated to their galleys, only to find that the ebbing tide had left them high on the beach. Furthermore, a detachment of MacLeods was standing guard over them. A small band succeeded in launching a boat and escaped, but the main body put up a last stand with their backs to a drystone dyke close by the beach. The MacDonalds were butchered to a man and the wall was tumbled down on top of them to obviate the necessity of burial. The battle was afterwards known as the Battle of the Spoiled Dyke.

In the old graveyard at Trumpan lies the grave of Lady Grange, a tragic victim of persecution. Her downfall was brought about because she overheard a Jacobite plot whilst hiding underneath a sofa. Stupidly, she accosted the plotters, her husband and his friends, and announced her intention of informing. Lord Grange and his fellow rebels resolved to keep her out of mischief. Over the years she had no less than three funerals! Initially she was bundled off to MacLeod territory in Skye, where she was installed in a primitive hut; news of her death was announced in Edinburgh and a mock funeral was held at Greyfriars Church. Then, after being held on the island of Heisker off North Uist for two years, she spent seven years on St.

The ruins of the old church at Trumpan. It was here that all the congregation were burned alive by the MacDonalds of Uist in 1578.

Dunvegan Castle, Skye, the seat of the Clan MacLeod. ►

The monument to the MacCrimmons at Borreraig on the ► ►
west shore of Loch Dunvegan.

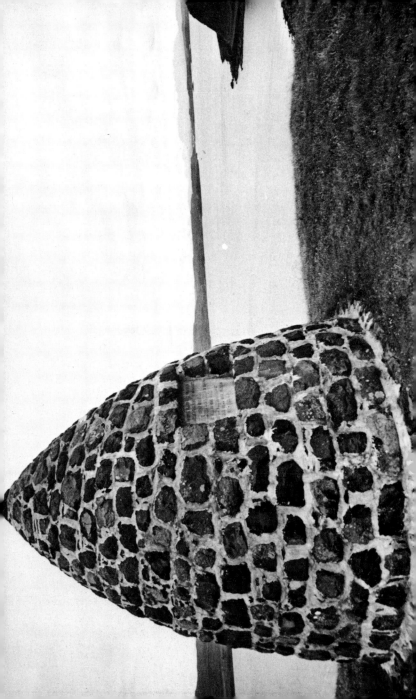

Kilda. Later she was taken back to Uist, then to Assynt on the mainland, and finally back to Skye. She eventually managed to send a letter to influential friends by hiding it in some yarn which she had spun, so a warship was sent to search the Skye coastline for her. At that time she was imprisoned in a sea cave on Loch Bracadale but it was considered a dangerous hiding place so she was put on a boat bound for Uist once more, escorted by a boatman who had a quick method of disposing of the lady, should a Government ship hove in sight. A running noose attached to a large boulder lay in the well of the boat for use in emergency! Eventually she was returned to Vaternish where she finally died in 1745. Her coffin was filled with turf and a second mock funeral was conducted at Duirinish, though her body was actually laid to rest at Trumpan churchyard.

Dunvegan, Loch Bracadale and Talisker

DUNVEGAN CASTLE ACTS as an historical magnet for visitors. MacLeods have lived here continuously for seven hundred years. The castle is built on the site of a ninth-century Norse fortress, perched on a crag and proudly facing the sea. It retains all the trappings of an ancient castle, cut off from land by a man-made moat (now spanned by a bridge), with nine foot thick walls to the keep and a suitably grim dungeon under the floor of the guardroom, covered by a flagstone trap. The dungeon is a vertical shaft sixteen feet deep by six feet wide and boasts an X-certificate history. Actually there were many good and kindly chiefs of the Clan MacLeod but, inevitably, the nasty ones provide better popular historical copy.

While the funeral of the ninth chief, John, was taking place, Ian Dubh took over Dunvegan Castle and, when the funeral party returned, murdered John's two brothers and three nephews, clapping the remainder of the party into the dungeons. Argyll (a Campbell) was the guardian of Mary, the dead chief's only child and he intervened on her behalf. After discussions between Ian Dubh and eleven of the Campbell chiefs an agreement was reached – or rather, the murderous new chief pretended to agree to Argyll's terms. A farewell feast was then held for the Campbells, towards the end of which they were served with goblets of blood. This was a sign for the Campbells to be dirked in their seats. The hated Ian Dubh kept the prisoners from the funeral party in the dungeon as hostages for the good behaviour of his clan and thus, for three years, held the estates. He was finally dislodged from his chieftainship by Norman, third son of Alasdair Crotach, who took over Dunvegan, aided by the Campbells and other powerful allies, and Ian's head warder, MacSween, who opened the gates for him. Ian himself escaped by a secret passage and eventually made his way to Ireland where, falling foul of a chief named O'Donnell, he was tortured and put to death with red hot irons thrust through his bowels.

Norman was unpopular for several reasons, not least for the obligation under which he had placed his clan towards Argyll, his Campbell patron. To strengthen his position as chief, he decided to despatch each of his male relatives, and all the descendants of John, as ninth chief. His leading henchmen were each allotted a victim and, under pain of death, were told to commit the murder on a certain day. This must have been quite an event, even for Dunvegan; John had had four daughters and twelve sons. With one exception, all of their descendants were killed. Needless to say, this last act did not endear Norman to his clan and, scared of being murdered himself, he formed a bodyguard of twelve thugs, each masterful in all forms of athletics and warfare. These hoods watched over him day and night and were called Buannachan (bullies). Their name was derived from the final aptitude test: that of

wrenching the leg of a bull off at the knee, with one hand.

Dunvegan Castle is open to the public and, as well as the Fairy Flag, there are many other objects of great interest on view, including the drinking horn of Rory Mor, reputed to have come from a wild bull killed by Rory in Glenelg. The horn holds five pints and at the inauguration of each new chief it has to be drained by him in a single draught. Modern chiefs, not possessing the same capacity as their forebears, have inserted a false bottom.

There are numerous places of interest in the immediate vicinity of Dunvegan. Two flat-topped hills, Healaval Bheag and Healaval Mhor, lying to the south-west, are known as MacLeod's Tables and are both easy and rewarding to climb. Alasdair Crotach was one of the greatest chiefs of his time. His name signifies "Hunchback", a deformity acquired when he was wounded between the shoulder blades with an axe. It was on the summit of one of these two peaks that Alasdair entertained a party of nobles. Once, visiting the King's palace in Edinburgh Alasdair had been teased that the dimensions of the royal table could not be matched on Skye. So he invited the party to the island to show them that his "table" was far greater – and a banquet was held on the summit!

Alasdair was the first chief to patronise the Mac-Crimmons, the hereditary pipers of the MacLeods. The

---

◄ *Loch Pooltiel and the cliffs of the western aspect of Dunvegan Head. From the cliff tops there are superb views to the Outer Isles on a clear day. North Uist is seen across the Minch.*

Skye's most westerly point, Neist lighthouse, in stately ►
solitude. A short way down the coast is Waterstein Head, a worthwhile walk to view the great cliffs.

MacLeod's Maidens, Idrigill Point on the western end of ► ►
Loch Bracadale.

famous MacCrimmon School of Piping was based across Loch Dunvegan at Borreraig where there is a memorial to commemorate it, and a new School of Piping has recently been inaugurated.

Much of the nearby coastline offers superb walks. The sea cliffs round Waterstein Head drop over 900ft to the Atlantic, punctuated by ribbon-like waterfalls which, in strong south-westerlies, can be seen to "fall" upwards. At the Duirinish side of Loch Bracadale stand several prominent women, MacLeod's Maidens, by name. These three hard ladies are sea stacks named after a mother and two daughters who lost their lives here. John, the third chief of the MacLeods was, to put it mildly, a man of uncontrollable temper. Two of his daughters wished to marry two brothers, the sons of one of his vassals. As he was unsuccessful in preventing the marriages, he buried his daughters alive in the dungeon of the castle and flogged the two brothers until "There was scarcely a spark of life left in them." Then he threw them over a precipice into the sea. Another time, out hunting, the stag which he had marked for himself was shot by one of his followers. He was so furious that he had the huntsman disembowelled on the spot with the antlers of the deer. Some relations of the murdered man killed the chief with an arrow as he was about to step into his galley (for the stalk had taken place on Harris). The boat, left unattended in the confusion, drifted away carrying his wife and daughters; it was driven before a strong wind and

---

◀ *Dun Beag broch, near Struan, Bracadale. The sea cliff on the left is Talisker Head. The point on the far right is close to the MacLeod's Maidens and the flat-topped hill to the right again is Healaval Bheag, one of MacLeod's Tables.*

The Mill, Glendale, Skye. ▶

Old croft outbuildings, Struan. ▶ ▶

eventually wrecked on the Maidens where the women perished. The best way to reach this point is to follow the coastline from Orbost.

On a fine spring day Loch Bracadale is one of those rare places which seems almost too perfect to be true. Beyond the islands the distant Cuillin rise in a jagged crown about a sea which can turn translucent blue-green. Above the road into Bracadale the ruined broch of Dun Beag offers a commanding view seawards to Idrigill Point and the Maidens, and to the gaunt, dark cliffs which lead round to Talisker Bay.

Talisker Bay is a forgotten place. To the south and east cliffs rise to 900ft constantly nibbled by the Atlantic swell; the boulder beach is a legacy of heavy seas. It has a harsh but fairyland quality about it. Boswell and Johnson stayed here on their visit to Skye. Johnson did not care for the wilder places of this world and Talisker was no exception; he wrote: "Talisker is the place beyond all that I have seen from which the gay and the jovial seem utterly excluded, and where the hermit might expect to grow old in meditation, without the possibility of disturbance or interruption."

Glen Brittle and the Black Cuillin

GLEN BRITTLE IS a Mecca for rock climbers. There is a Youth Hostel, and also a camp site by the beach. The Black Cuillin offer more exposed rock – good solid rock at that – than any other range in Britain and the traverse of the Cuillin ridge must be the finest single mountaineering expedition in the British Isles: a total of 10,000ft (3,048m) of ascent across its crazy profile. The average time for completing the ridge is nine to twelve hours but if Clach Glas and Blaven are included, a further four to six hours are required. The first complete traverse in a day was made in 1939; the first winter

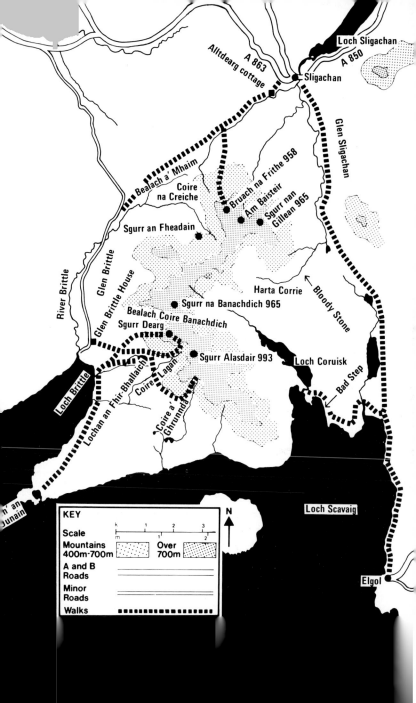

Loch Sligachan

A 850

A 863

Alltdearg cottage

Sligachan

Glen Sligachan

Bealach a' Mhaim

Coire na Creiche

Bruach na Frithe 958

Am Basteir

Sgurr nan Gillean 965

Sgurr an Fheadain

Glen Brittle

River Brittle

Glen Brittle House

Harta Corrie

Bloody Stone

Sgurr na Banachdich 965

Bealach Coire Banachdich

Sgurr Dearg

Coire Lagan

Sgurr Alasdair 993

Loch Coruisk

Bad Step

Lochan an Fhir-Bhallaich

Coire a' Ghrunnda

Loch Brittle

n an
unain

Loch Scavaig

Elgol

KEY

Scale

k .... 1 .... 2 3
m 1 2

Mountains
400m-700m   **Over 700m**

A and B Roads

Minor Roads

Walks

N

traverse in 1965. It is no country, however, for the novice to wander nonchalantly. Many of the peaks are out of reach of the inexperienced and the summits which I have mentioned as suitable for the average fit person can be hazardous in mist. It is no use being prepared to sit it out – the cloud has been known to remain for a month!

Where the road descends the hill into Glen Brittle, a path angles in from the left. This is the track which leads over the Bealach a' Mhaim (now afforested) to Alltdearg cottage, close to Sligachan. Coire na Creiche is well viewed from the Glen Brittle road: a wide desolate basin. Rising behind it is the pointed head of Sgurr an Fheadain, cleft by Waterpipe Gully, as if by a Lochaber axe. It was in Coire na Creiche (Corrie of the Spoils) that the last clan battle was fought in 1601 between the age-long rivals, the MacDonalds and the MacLeods. Until recent times the graves of those killed in this battle were visible on the floor of the corrie.

This battle was the culmination of several years of pillage and plunder and is known as the War of the One-Eyed Woman. It was common practice at that period to contract a conjugal agreement known as handfasting; in modern terms, a trial marriage. The chief of the MacDonalds of Duntulm obtained the sister of the chief of the MacLeods of Dunvegan and took her off to his stronghold "on approval". But Margaret MacLeod received an eye injury, after which Donald Gorm Mor deemed her substandard for his wife, so at the termination of a year and a day – the verbal terms of the handfast contract – he returned the goods to Dunvegan. In order to make the reason for his

---

Glen Drynoch and the Cuillin. Sgurr nan Gillean is the ▶
snowy peak, far left. Coire na Creiche is the corrie above
the house in centre and the Carbost – Glen Brittle road
goes over the Drynoch Bridge, left of centre. Old lazybeds
can be seen centre and right.

refusal abundantly clear, he mounted her on an ancient one-eyed nag, led by a one-eyed groom with a one-eyed dog in the train.

Before the battle began, the MacDonalds had made an extensive cattle raid and the crags of the corrie were echoing with the lowing of MacLeod black cattle as the MacLeods arrived hot for revenge. The battle of Coire na Creiche was won by the MacDonalds and part of their victorious song runs:

> One day I happed in rocky Cuillin,
> I heard the great warpipe astrumming,
> Lowing of milch kine responding . . .

Back in Edinburgh, however, James VI was worried in case news of this battle leaked out and prejudiced the chances of his claim to the English throne as James I, so he ordered both of the chiefs to be held in custody whilst a peace was negotiated. A feast of pacification was held at Dunvegan and there was much celebration. As a contemporary bard put it:

> Twenty times drunk were we each day,
> Nor did we rebel against it any more than he.

Considering its proximity to such magnificent surroundings, Glen Brittle is a rather nondescript glen, despite the great wall of the Cuillin rising on its easterly doorstep. From the beach the shoreline reaches out to either side of the loch as if to embrace the island of Canna. It is worth remembering that these two points often attract better weather in the "rainy season". The southerly point is of especial interest as there is a ruined dun and horned cairn here; there is

---

◄ *Coire na Creiche at the head of Glen Brittle. This is the site of the last clan battle in Scotland, during the War of the One-Eyed Woman.*

also a small inland loch with an obviously artificial channel leading to the sea. Perhaps this sheltered lochan too was used by the MacAskills for their birlinns. The clan is supposed to have occupied Rubh' an Dunain for as long as the MacLeods occupied Dunvegan. A MacAskill was always the hereditary coast-watcher for the MacLeods and one sailed as commodore with the chief in his galley. Now only ruined crofts remain inland from the old dun, yet in these humble quarters great men were born. One such became the Governor of Mauritius and another, Major General Sir John MacAskill, was a distinguished soldier.

Two paths climbing the grassy hillside from Glen Brittle serve as a means of access to the Cuillin from the west. To reach Coire Lagan, take either the track from the beach or that from Glen Brittle House to Lochan an Fhir-Bhallaich (Loch of the Speckled Trout). At the far side of the lochan follow the higher path that rises into the corrie which, like other rock basins in the Cuillin, was probably formed in the later stages of the Ice Age, gouged out by the action of corrie glaciers; the smooth pebble-scratched slabs are very conspicuous here.

The ascent of Sgurr Dearg (3,209ft/979m) from Glen Brittle gives a worthwhile, if energetic, day. Again, the approach can be made either from behind Glen Brittle House or by taking the path from the beach up Sron Dearg to the summit. Care should be exercised near the top where some rock scrambling is required. The Inaccessible Pinnacle which is at the summit of Sgurr Dearg is partly gabbro, sandwiched between two dykes.

◄ *Sgurr Dearg from Glen Brittle. The route to the summit takes the foreground ridge, which can be gained either from the beach or from Glen Brittle House. The Bealach Coire Banachdich is the saddle to the left of the peak and should be reached from the corrie.*

The Inaccessible Pinnacle, Sgurr Dearg, from the east. ►

The Inaccessible Pinnacle from the top of Sgurr Dearg. ► ►

It is perched on a dolerite sheet and its ascent should be left to those with rock climbing experience. It forms the second highest point on Skye, Sgurr Alasdair across Coire Lagan being the highest (3,257ft/993m). Sgurr Dearg is a tremendous viewpoint; on a good day the Outer Isles stretch in convoy way beyond the Minch. Loch Coruisk is hidden from here but across Coire Lagan is the great rock face of Sron na Ciche, one of the largest continuous faces of gabbro in the Cuillin. The next peak to the north of Sgurr Dearg is Sgurr na Banachdich and between is Bealach Coire Banachdich which provides a gateway over the divide to Loch Coruisk from Glen Brittle. The descent from Sgurr Dearg should be made by the route of ascent, or by dropping down into Coire Lagan. The path to this corrie skirts the Pinnacle on its southern side, angles down, then traverses to the head of the Stone Shoot. It is dangerous to strike off right too early – keep to the path! A well-marked trail leads from Coire Lagan back to Glen Brittle.

To climb Sgurr Alasdair, there is for the walker but one route of ascent up the great treadmill of the Stone Shoot. The peak is appropriately named for it was first ascended by Sheriff Alexander Nicholson of Portree. Nicholson was a great lover of the Cuillin and his *History of Skye* should be read by anyone with an interest in this fascinating island. The great pyramid of Sgurr Alasdair towers above the dark mirror of the lochan, and screes rise in toilsome disarray to the high surrounding crags. The top of the Alasdair Stone Shoot is only a little way from the summit and a short rocky scramble takes one onto it. The mountain is separate from the main Cuillin divide but this in no way detracts from it as a vantage point. There is an eagle's eye view of Coire Lagan far below. Behind, the solitude of Coire a' Ghrunnda beckons; being further from Glen Brittle it is less frequented than Coire Lagan. The route back to Glen Brittle is again by the Stone Shoot, easier on descent, though with the passage of time and boots, the movement of smaller scree to the depths of the corrie means one can no longer scree-run the Shoot with dignity.

On the left, from Coire Lagan, the huge gabbro wall of Sron na Ciche forms a 1,000-foot rampart. This is a popular playground for rock climbers and dozens of routes criss-cross its flanks. By looking carefully, the outline of the Cioch (the Breast) may be spotted or, in the afternoon, its shadow may be seen projected across the expanse of the Cioch Slab. The Cioch was first detected by its shadow by the late Professor Norman Collie who later climbed it. Like its colleague, the Inaccessible Pinnacle of Sgurr Dearg, it is best left to the attentions of rock climbers.

The same path which leads up to the Lochan an Fhir-Bhallaich continues across the slopes below Coire Lagan to the bottom of the Sron na Ciche face, where another branch swings right to the next corrie – Coire a' Ghrunnda – by traversing round the end of Sron na Ciche. More scrambling is required to gain this corrie which bears the indelible stamp of the Ice Age and is of considerable interest to geologists as well as to the walker.

Half a mile west of Sligachan is the other end of the track that links Sligachan with the Glen Brittle road. Going west the path starts at Alltdearg cottage and leads over the Bealach a' Mhaim. The road leading to the Allt Dearg is private but there is a good car park at the road end. The path cuts off right just before the cottage, then accompanies the stream on its true left bank.

The great cliffs of Sron na Ciche. The Cioch can be seen ►
casting a shadow over the Cioch Slab. The east shore of Loch Brittle is on the right and just past the lochan, at the point, is a dun.

The Inaccessible Pinnacle from the north side of Sgurr ► ►
Mhic Coinnich. Bealach Coire Banachdich is the col to the right of centre and the easiest pass from Glen Brittle to Loch Coruisk.

An ascent of Bruach na Frithe (3,143ft/958m) can also be made from this path. It is one of the easiest peaks in the Cuillin and is a good place from which to view the ridge and corries on the south side. Cross the Allt Dearg beyond the waterfall if it is not in spate, and travel over rough ground – there is no path – to gain the long, easy nose which eventually leads up to the main divide. On the left rises the jagged outline of the Pinnacle Ridge of Sgurr nan Gillean (the Peak of the Young Men). The great fang of rock near the point where the crest is gained is the Bhasteir Tooth (3,005ft/916m) which creates one of the major obstacles when traversing the main ridge from south to north. Shadowing it is Am Baisteir (the Executioner). The small pass close by the Tooth is known as Bealach nan Lice (Pass of the Flat Stone).

Though the ascent of Bruach na Frithe is possibly the easiest of any peak in the Black Cuillin, even this can be treacherous in cloud. A strenuous but uneventful walk up can, under mist, turn into a hazardous descent. With this in mind, a compass and map should be carried, as indeed on all the walks.

◀ *Coire Lagan and the Great Stone Shoot (the white line) leading up to Sgurr Alasdair. The Isle of Soay is seen above the Sron na Ciche, with Muck and Rhum.*

The path can be seen descending from the summit of ▶ *Sgurr Dearg to the stone shoot, which leads to Coire Lagan. It should be noted that in mist this path can be dangerous, for any deviation from it can immediately lead on to hazardous ground. The photograph is taken from the top of Sgurr Alasdair stone shoot.*

The Cioch with Loch Brittle. The path to Coire Lagan ▶ ▶ *passes the small lochan just above the top of the Cioch and is seen here to the right of the Cioch as it starts to climb into Coire Lagan. It should be noted that the Cioch can only be reached by rock climbers.*

Glen Sligachan offers a long trek if its length is traversed to the shores of Loch Scavaig and then on to Elgol. This is the route Prince Charlie took on his final walk on Skye. After his brief stay on Raasay he had returned to Skye in the role of male servant to Malcolm MacLeod, a cousin of Young Raasay who had been a captain of the Prince's at Culloden. Though Malcolm was very fit, the Prince was even fitter, and having to remain a respectable distance behind his newly appointed lord and master, and walking at a slower place than normal, sorely tried the Prince's patience. All the sustenance he and his companion had for the last stage of their journey – thirty miles – was a bottle of brandy. The bogs of Glen Sligachan would have been as squelchy then as today. According to a contemporary report, when he arrived at the house of John Mac-Kinnon (who took him to the mainland in his boat) his feet were washed by an old crone, a common custom after a long walk, and she was heard to exclaim in disgust, "Filthy fellow!"

◄ *Coire a' Ghrunnda with the Isles of Soay, Rhum and Eigg top left. The path, which involves some rock scrambling, gains the corrie to the right of the lochan. The helicopter parked at the water's edge gives an appreciation of the scale.*

Sgurr nan Gillean on the left. The left-hand ridge of the ► *next peak to the right, which looks similar to Sgurr nan Gillean, gives access to the west side of the Bhasteir Tooth and Bruach na Frithe. The path from Alltdearg comes in from the left and the Sligachan-Glen Brittle path cuts across the darker ground below the peaks.*

The pinnacle ridge of Sgurr nan Gillean from near ► ► *Bruach na Frithe.*

Glen Carron and over the hills to Torridon

THE ISLANDS OF Raasay and Skye shelter the Loch Carron and Applecross coastline from the ravages of the Atlantic. To the north lies the more rugged country of the north-west seaboard, a region deficient in arable ground but possessing a surplus of rock.

Northwards from Kyle of Lochalsh, the coastal fringe of Balmacara is peppered with a host of islands and skerries and along this shore runs the picturesque Kyle of Lochalsh railway, hugging the edge of Loch Carron on its journey from Garve. For part of the way the road from Kintail to Strathcarron keeps it company.

Plockton is regarded by some as a "white settlers" village. Certainly, a high proportion of the houses are owned by holidaymakers, but this in no way detracts from its simple appeal. At Loch Kishorn is the site of an oil platform yard, which revitalised an ailing rural economy to the detriment of one of the most scenic regions of Scotland.

There is a shortage of interesting walks into the hinterland to the south side of Loch Carron. But near the head of the loch, close to the mouth of the River Attadale, an estate road cuts deeply into the hills as far as Bendronaig Lodge. This gives a long and invigorating walk and it is possible to take an alternative route back to Strathcarron by following the hill track from the west side of Black Water, over Bealach Altan Ruairidh. By the Eas Ban stream another track branches off left in a south-westerly direction to join the Attadale track. The other continues roughly north-west, eventually dropping down to Achintee and Strathcarron.

At the head of Loch Carron the road divides. The left branch follows the north shore of the loch to Loch-carron village, sometimes referred to as Jeanstown.

◀ *The north face of Am Basteir (the Executioner) with the Tooth on the right.*

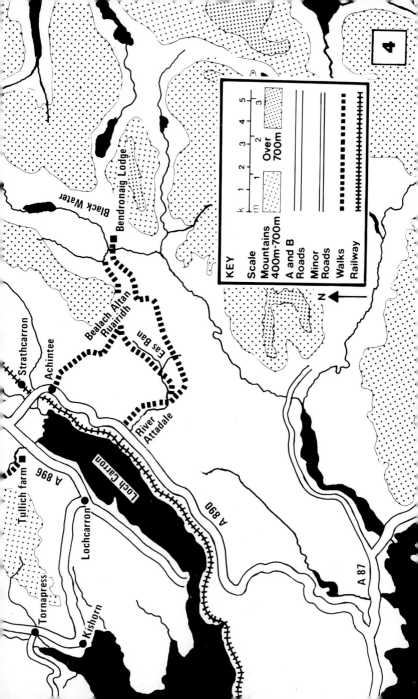

4

KEY

Scale

Mountains
400m–700m

A and B
Roads

Minor
Roads

Walks

Railway

Over
700m

N

Strathcarron

Achintee

Bealach Alltan Ruairidh

Bendronaig Lodge

Black Water

Eas Ban

River Attadale

Tullich farm

A 896

Loch Carron

Lochcarron

A 890

Tornapress

Kishorn

A 87

The right-hand fork leads up Glen Carron to Achnasheen (Field of Rain). The only redeeming features of this settlement which includes two hotels and a railway station are the roads and railway leading out of it.

Glen Carron is the springboard for a wonderland of peaks and glens to the north and west. Achnashellach station is not the most conspicuously signposted frontier of British Rail, but once found it offers an excellent point of departure into the barrier of hills stretching to Glen Torridon in the north and to Applecross in the west. The glens and bens of this region are obligingly served by good paths.

The twelve-mile walk over the Coulin Pass, from Achnashellach to Kinlochewe, is superb, following an A 1 path which was an old clan highway. The journey can be shortened by continuing on the main Coulin track to the Torridon road at Loch Clair. The walk starts at Achnashellach station from a gate on the north side of the line and takes the forest road to the Coulin Pass at 950 feet. At Coulin, cross the river to Torrancuilinn; 250 yards beyond you can either head north to Kinlochewe, or follow the east shore of Loch Clair to the Torridon road as already mentioned.

An alternative to the Coulin walk also starts at Achnashellach station, this time from the small gate just west of the station on the north side. This path follows the River Lair; firstly through pines, then up the true left of the river to emerge onto a flat expanse of open ground at Loch Coire Lair. The main path continues on north of the loch, but the alternative to the Coulin Pass now branches off right (north-east) to join up with the Coulin track at the Easan Dorcha. Then, of course, the Coulin Pass can be traversed north to south to make this a round trip.

At the junction of the paths by the River Lair it is also feasible to cross the river (unless it is in spate) and follow a good track which leads on to Bealach Mhor,

between Mainreachan Buttress of Fuar Tholl and Sgorr Ruadh (3,142ft/957m). Mainreachan is a great rock tombstone with climbs of over 700 feet up its northern face. The whole surrounding region is one of wild splendour. Here the mountains have elbow room and good paths linking them, built originally as pony tracks for deer stalking.

From Bealach Mhor there are a number of possibilities for the hill walker. Firstly there is Sgorr Ruadh – to the right as you reach the pass – offering an easy ascent to its summit by following the gentle, sweeping ridge. Alternatively, the traverse of Fuar Tholl (2,975ft/907m) can be made by taking the skyline ridge from the bealach over the top of Mainreachan. Fuar Tholl means the Cold Hole, a name probably earned for its snow-holding capacity. It is, literally, a cold mountain. The descent route is to the south, then eastwards back to Achnashellach station.

The path that continues along the bank of the River Lair and into the corrie crosses over the divide into Torridon. From the floor of Coire Lair you can ascend to 1,900ft (588m) over the pass which lies between Sgorr Ruadh and Beinn Liath Mhor (3,034ft/925m). One then slants westward round the northerly shoulder of Sgorr Ruadh to gain a second pass, Bealach Ban (1,650ft/503m). The slopes of Meall Dearg are then traversed to the south-west towards the Bealach na Lice where the path skirts the north-east shore of Loch an Eoin. It then leads across the lower north-eastern slopes of Beinn na h-Eaglaise and finally down to Annat, on the shore of Loch Torridon. This walk, covering about ten miles, provides an energetic but rewarding day.

It is possible to join up with the Achnashellach–Annat walk by taking a track from Coulags, some three

---

◄ Fuar Tholl, with Mainreachan Buttress to the left, and on the right, Sgorr Ruadh with Bealach Mhor between.

miles south-west of Achnashellach on the main road. Initially, the track follows the true left of the Fionn-abhainn; after a mile it crosses the river and follows its course up to Loch Coire Fionnaraich, leaving this loch on the right to climb towards Bealach na Lice (1,300ft/ 396m). It is twelve miles to Annat if the route from Bealach na Lice is followed via Loch an Eoin (as in the Achnashellach–Annat walk). A less strenuous round tour can be made by cutting north-east over Bealach Ban from Bealach na Lice to drop down into Coire Lair and thence by the riverside path to Achnashellach.

From Tullich farm, close to the head of Loch Carron, a track leads over the Bealach a'Ghlas-chnoic (1,350ft/ 412m) to reach the Kishorn–Shieldaig road, the A896, at Loch an Loin. For those with some hill walking experience, it is also possible to head north-east from the Bealach a'Ghlas-chnoic and traverse the great expanse of rocky hillside to climb An Ruadh-stac (2,919ft/890m). From the summit of this peak there are fine views of Beinn Damph and Upper Loch Torridon; a descent should be made eastwards to reach the path which approaches from the Fionn-abhainn, half a mile south of Loch Coire Fionnaraich. From here the Fionn-abhainn glen can be followed back to the main road at Coulags. In event of bad visibility, all walks which include summits in this region to the north of Glen Carron should be avoided as there is an over-abundance of cliffs.

◄ *Mainreachan Buttress, Fuar Tholl, from close to the path to Bealach Mhor.*

A high road into Applecross

APPLECROSS, AS SEEN from the road near Kishorn, is an imposing, castellated landscape of Torridonian sandstone. It possesses a faintly unreal, fairytale quality so that once the Bealach na Ba (Pass of the Cattle) is climbed you do indeed seem to enter another world: a world more gentle, where the whole tempo of life beats more slowly.

The Bealach na Ba permits entry from the south and has recently been linked to the northern end of the peninsula by a new coastal road which emerges close to Shieldaig. The road over the bealach is the highest in Western Scotland, reaching a height of 2,053ft (625m) in only six miles. On the eastern side of the pass the road is flanked by sandstone precipices. But even before the pass is gained there are several walks worth attention. At Tornapress, Loch Kishorn, where the Bealach na Ba road commences, a stalker's path starting from a stone hut follows above the river on the western side. The path should be followed as far as the burn descending from Coire na Feola. Here a small track accompanying the stream takes one up to the lip of the corrie allowing a fine view of this great amphitheatre. By continuing northwards over rough ground two other magnificent corries can also be visited: Coire na Poite and Coire nan Fhamhair.

A fine walk, which takes full advantage of the height climbed by the road, starts at the Bealach na Ba. It involves some three miles of fairly rough going and a thousand feet of climbing. Rather than head for the obvious skyline (where the transmitting mast can be seen) a more direct line should be taken for the left-hand col by descending first into the large corrie; then

Beinn Bhan, Applecross, Coire nan Fhamhair. ▶

The Russel Burn close to the Bealach na Ba road. Behind ▶ ▶
is the Cioch of Sgurr a' Chaorachain.

following the track over Bealach nan Arr to the Beinn Bhan cairn. From the top one has a raven's eye view of the great corries of Beinn Bhan.

After viewing the corries the route can be retraced or, alternatively, it is possible to descend into Coire nan Fhamhair, taking the easiest line from the low point, or by traversing round on top of the peak embracing the corrie to the north, to descend by its easy east ridge. The stalker's path can be picked up to the east of Lochan Coire na Poite and thence to Tornapress. It should be noted that in the event of snow, poor visibility, or high winds, these high routes should be avoided; even in good weather some basic knowledge of mountain walking is desirable.

A less demanding, though rewarding, walk (returning the same way) leaving the road to the pass at Russel Bridge, takes a path on the true right of the Russel Burn into Coire nan Arr. Here, rising like a gigantic broch, is the Cioch or pap of Sgurr a' Chaorachain. The ascent of the Cioch – though not hard in rock climbing terms – is one of the classical routes in the Western Highlands.

Descending on the west side of the Bealach na Ba one leaves the austere wildness of the exposed Torridonian sandstone to discover the lush beauty of the coast. From the right bank of the Applecross River, a track cuts across to Shieldaig (nine miles), firstly by a rough road, then by a path which in one mile forks. The northern, left-hand track goes six miles to Kenmore, whilst the other carries on over a pass of 1,213ft (369m) to the south of Croic-bheinn. Here the path again divides; the best choice is that leading north-north-east to Inverbain where the road to Shieldaig is joined.

◄ *The corries of Beinn Bhan, Applecross.*

Loch Kishorn and the hills of Applecross. The Cioch is ►
the prominent rocky peak above the hut.

A view from the church across Loch Kishorn to Sgurr a' ► ►
Chaorachain and the Cioch.

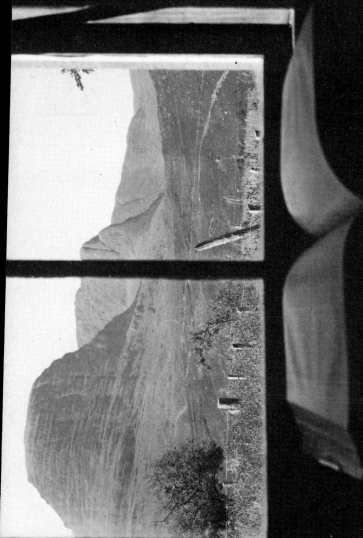

Two miles south of Applecross village is Camus-terrach, sheltered by Eilean nan Naomh (the Holy Isle) where, it is reputed, St. Maelrubha landed in 673. He declared the spot a sanctuary and it remained one until the Reformation. The bounds of the sanctuary were marked by a six-mile arc of stones which have long since disappeared. The most southerly one – an eight-foot high cross – stood on a promontory close to Camusterrach. All traces of St. Maelrubha's church have now vanished, razed by Viking raids in the ninth and tenth centuries. The old name of the whole peninsula was Comeraich, meaning "Sanctuary".

Until recently there was only a track linking Apple-cross with the crofting communities in the northern sector of the peninsula. Now a road steals along this shoreline, destroying a remoteness which is irreplace-able. Yet, provided the landowners are amenable, it may revitalise an old way of life where land was utilised to the full, albeit in modest ways. The villages of Fearnmore and Fearnbeg give a unique insight into that way of life: a life not dictated by time of the clock, but rather by seasons and the weather.

Shieldaig nestles in the arms of Loch Shieldaig like a contented pensioner. The village has an air of repose; sheep wander along its one street and boats rest be-tween outings. Tucked away from the main road, and reached from the south through gnarled Caledonian pines, the village seems more genuine than Plockton to the south, with which comparison seems inevitable. A walk to the point past Camas-ruadh is well worthwhile. It is only a little over a mile and, on a good day, fine views are obtained up Upper Loch Torridon to the

---

◄ *Meall Gorm and Loch Kishorn from a bridge on the Bealach na Ba road.*

The Cioch, Applecross. ►

Looking towards Kishorn from above the Bealach na Ba road. ► ►

hills, and westwards along the shore of Loch Torridon itself.

To the east of Shieldaig the new road cuts above the coastline to Glen Torridon. From the Balgy Burn the old footpath can be followed past the two idyllic inlets– Ob Gorm Beag and Ob Gorm Mor – then continuing through superb woods to Loch Torridon Hotel where the new road is rejoined. This track is part of the old clan route shown in Roy's map of 1755.

From across the main road at Loch Torridon Hotel a stalker's path strikes up the hill. By following it up through a scenic gorge, Beinn Damph (2,957ft/901m) can be climbed without difficulty, heading first towards the saddle between it and Sgurr na Bana Mhoraire (2,254ft/687m).

▲ ◄ *The Bealach na Ba road. In the background to the right is the Beinn Bhan massif.*

◄ *A black house, still in use in Applecross.*

Fearnmore, Applecross. Craig, on the north shore of Loch ► ▲ *Torridon, is above the left chimney.*

Loch Torridon with the hills of the Letterewe Forest ► *beyond, from the north shore of Applecross.*

Shieldaig with the peaks of Torridon behind. ► ► ▲

Upper Loch Torridon with Liathach on the left and Beinn ► ► *Damph on the right. Between are the peaks of the Coulin and Beinn Damph Forests.*

Beinn Alligin, Liathach and Beinn Eighe

THE NORTH SIDE of Glen Torridon is under the benevolent care of the National Trust for Scotland and there
are no restrictions during the stalking season. The road
forks at the head of the loch and the main road continues up through Glen Torridon to Kinlochewe,
whilst a side road leads through the village of Fasag and
follows the shoreline as far as the Torridon House road
end, at the foot of Coire Mhic Nobuil. It then rises
through pine woods to follow the shoulder of the hill,
high above Inver Alligin, to terminate at Diabaig.
However, it is possible to travel on foot, keeping to the
shore for most of the way, to Inver Alligin and then on
to Diabaig via Port Laire (which consists of one cottage!) On a good day this is one of the finest walks in the
Highlands and arrival at Diabaig – a gem of a village –
is ample reward for the effort. The journey can be
shortened by taking car, or bus, to Inver Alligin, thereby saving several miles. From Diabaig itself one can
also continue to the Youth Hostel at Craig and on to
Red Point over a good path, passing the salmon fishing
station on the way. This walk ends at Redpoint farm, at
the termination of the road running south from Port
Henderson. It must be left to the ingenuity of the
walker to find his lift home . . .

From the car park at the Coire Mhic Nobuil burn
there are several other interesting excursions. For
example, the ascent of Beinn Alligin (3,232ft/985m) –
the Jewel Mountain – offers no great problems if a
return by the same described line is adhered to. The
shoulder of the mountain should be taken by following
a path which gains the mouth of Coire an Laoigh and

Upper Loch Torridon with Inver Alligin on the far shore. ▶
*The footpath from Balgy to Loch Torridon Hotel runs
hidden across the foreground.*

Fasag, Upper Loch Torridon. ▶ ▶

the stream is then followed to its source. On the sky-line, head for the summit of Tom na Gruagaich (3,024ft/921m). From this summit a wide panorama opens, the great gash of Sgurr Mhor prominent in this view.

Alternatively, ascend Sgurr Mhor whose summit offers superb views of the surrounding country. The Coire Mhic Nobuil path should be taken as far as the Allt Toll a' Mhadaidh, then follow the burn up through boulders and heather to gain the summit.

Also from the Coire Mhic Nobuil car park the round of Liathach makes a long but rewarding tramp. Follow the Coire Mhic Nobuil path to its end, then continue on past Loch Grobaig and Lochan a' Choire Dhuibh. Another path is encountered running south down Coire Dubh to Glen Torridon. This gives a walk of some eight miles, but of course leaves car users the problem of getting back to their starting point.

From Lochan a' Choire Dhuibh a path contours northwards round Sail Mhor into Coire Mhic Fhear-chair, one of the grandest corries in Scotland. It can also be reached in a separate excursion from the car park in upper Glen Torridon; this walk takes about two hours. The Triple Buttress of Coire Mhic Fhearchair stands boldly out, like three giants resting their sandstone feet just above the loch, whilst their quartzite heads are often enshrouded by cloud. These buttresses provide climbs for mountaineers in both summer and winter, as the gullies on the face hold snow until springtime. By following the burn from Loch Coire Mhic Fhear-chair a stalker's path can be picked up on the left which provides a good descent to Grudie Bridge on Loch Maree.

To the far left of the Triple Buttress a col will be

◄ *Craig Youth Hostel.*

Upper Loch Torridon with Beinn Alligin right of centre. ►

Liathach, the Grey One. ► ►

seen. This provides an easy scramble to gain the west end of the ridge of Beinn Eighe.

The traverse of Beinn Eighe demands a long day on the hill. Should no transport be available to take one back to base, a walk of some twenty miles is involved – not to mention the ascent and descent! It can be tackled either from the Kinlochewe end or from Coire Mhic Fhearchair via the stone shoot, as already mentioned. There are various obstacles to those with no hill walking or rock scrambling experience, especially round the Black Carls and the rock step between the top of Mhic Fhearchair and Sail Mhor. The quartzite when wet can be very treacherous and great care should be exercised. Should the traverse prove too long there are various easy lines of descent to the Torridon–Kinlochewe road. From Creag Dubh, the last peak when going west to east, you can drop down either to Cromasaig or to Anancaun.

▲ ◄ ◄ *The harbour, Diabaig.*

◄ ◄ *The north side of Liathach with Coire na Caime as seen from the path to Coire Mhic Fhearchair.*

▲ ◄ *Coire Mhic Fhearchair.*

◄ *Liathach and Beinn Eighe from Loch Clair.*

Beinn Eighe from Allt a'Chuirn. ►

Beinn Eighe from the north. ► ►

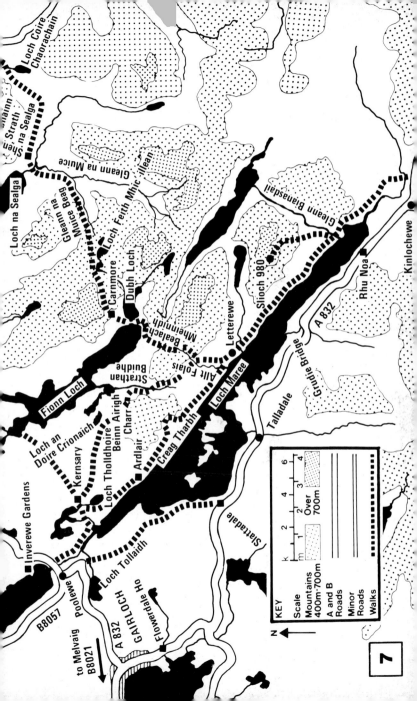

Kinlochewe and Loch Maree

THE NATURE CONSERVANCY Council run a residential field station at Anancaun farmhouse, close to Kinlochewe. Almost 11,000 acres of the eastern section of Beinn Eighe were bought in 1951 and it was actually the first Nature Reserve to be created. There is a Nature Trail where, if lucky, you may see pine marten, wild cat, or golden eagle.

Kinlochewe is a good base for both the traverse of Beinn Eighe and for an ascent of Slioch (3,217ft/980m). The name is derived from Sleigh, a spear. The easiest line of ascent is by the south-east ridge; the problem lies in reaching its base, which involves either making a five-mile hike round the head of Loch Maree to Gleann Bianasdail, or arranging to be ferried across from the south-east end of Loch Maree from Rhu Noa.

The old right of way to Poolewe can be followed past Gleann Bianasdail and along the north shore of Loch Maree. It is possible for those who are fit to make the trip from Kinlochewe to Poolewe in one day. This gives a beautiful but strenuous walk of nineteen miles, well away from the traffic of the south-west shore. The track (which keeps to the margin of the loch) was used to carry the mail for the Western Isles to Poolewe before the Inverness-to-Lochalsh railway was opened. The path continues past Letterewe Estate where a private ferry runs across the loch to the south shore. Close to Letterewe House iron was discovered and worked in the early 1700s and the surrounding forest was felled for iron smelting. The path skirts the margin of the loch at Creag Tharbh and beyond, in a detour, it picks its way higher up the hillside to reach Ardlair. Then it turns northwards by the west side of Loch Tholldhoire. At Kernsary it meets up with an estate road which leads down to Inveran and Poolewe.

◄ *Inland from Talladale, a view toward Baosbheinn.*
Loch Maree and Slioch.
Looking across Loch Maree from above Letterewe. ► ►

The path by the Allt Folais can be taken from Letterewe. After about a mile it forks. The right branch climbs over the Bealach Mheinnidh, then drops down to the causeway between Dubh Loch and Fionn Loch, at the far side of which is Carnmore Lodge and bothy. It is as well to be prepared to camp as there is no guarantee that the bothy will be available, and it certainly will not be during the stalking season. Permission to camp or to use the bothy should be obtained from the Estate factor. The left-hand branch of the path crosses the Allt Folais and goes north-west, parallel with Loch Maree, to the divide. It then heads northwards down Strathan Buidhe, skirts round Beinn Airigh Charr and on to Kernsary. The section of this path alongside Beinn Airigh Charr is the popular route into Carnmore from Kernsary, but in places is not well defined and provides strenuous walking.

The walk from Kinlochewe to Carnmore via Letterewe and the Bealach Mheinnidh is one of the finest in the British Isles and also one of the most remote. An overnight stay in this wilderness area is a unique experience, for there are few places anywhere to equal the grandeur of Carnmore.

From Carnmore it is possible to go on to Dundonnell. The path climbs steeply eastwards above Dubh Loch, follows the bank of a stream north-east to Lochan Feith Mhic'-illean, then turns east again, descending Gleann na Muice Beag to reach Gleann na Muice. Once the stream, Abhainn Strath na Sealga, is met it must be forded (hazardous in wet weather for it is deep). Shenavall bothy lies on the northern bank. It is possible to use Shenavall, except during the stalking season. Some two and a half miles upstream the path to the Dundonnell road climbs out of the glen and leads

◀ *The Letterewe Forest from Poolewe.*
The causeway Fionn Loch and Dubh Loch, Carnmore. ▶
Carnmore Lodge, below Torr na h'Iolaire, left of centre. ▶ ▶
The path to Shenavall goes up rightwards from the lodge.
Fionn Loch is hidden in left foreground.

northwards past Loch Coire Chaorachain. The total distance involved is twenty-three miles from Kinlochewe to Dundonnell.

As mentioned earlier, this walk can also be done from Poolewe. The road from Poolewe to Kernsary is private, but permission to drive along it can be obtained from the factor, Letterewe Estate. After passing Kernsary farm the road is followed round a wooded hillside leading to a hollow. Go through a gate and a short way beyond a cairn denotes the start of an elusive path running off to the right. The path meets the true right of the stream, which follows directly up the valley towards the foot of the conspicuous buttress of Martha's Peak which is the northern top of Beinn Airigh Charr. After the shoulder is reached you should avoid moving left, but cross a small flat area with no obvious path, then descend to an ill-defined track leading to Loch an Doire Crionaich. Pass the loch on its northern side to enjoy a good path. Poolewe to Dundonnell is twenty-eight miles. The boathouse at Fionn Loch can also be reached via Kernsary; Fionn Loch is one of the best trout lochs in the Scottish Highlands; Osgood MacKenzie, the creator of Inverewe Gardens, recorded a catch here of a dozen trout weighing eighty-eight lbs. Even today the fishing is exceptional.

Loch Maree was given its name more than a thousand years ago, after the Irish saint, Maelrubha. He had a cell on the tiny island in the loch called Eilean Ma-Ruibhe (now usually referred to as Isle Maree). It was common practice for these early Christian saints to incorporate aspects of Druid worship into their teachings, as well as utilising the pagan sites of worship: on

◀ *On Bealach Mheinnidh, between Letterewe and Fionn Loch, heading north.*

In the background Beinn Lair, with the Bealach Mheinnidh on the right. Carnmore Lodge is in the foreground with the path leading to the causeway between Fionn Loch and Dubh Loch. ▶

Red Point, the outermost point of Loch Torridon. ▶ ▶

Iona, for example, and also at Applecross where the remains of St. Maelrubha were buried. Eilean Ma-Ruibhe was also a place of pagan rites; as late as 1678 bulls were sacrificed on the island. According to the church records in Dingwall, members of the Mac-Kenzie family appeared before the Presbytery charged with this offence. There was at one time a sacred well on the island, reputedly with great powers of healing, but it has long since dried up.

The Loch Maree Hotel at Talladale is famed for its fishing: sea trout of up to twenty lbs have been caught between July 1st and mid-October, and salmon from April to May.

Two miles beyond Loch Maree Hotel, at Slattadale, a path cuts over the hills north and west to join up with the Gairloch-Poolewe road at Tollaidh. This five-mile walk starts from the forest car park where the walk is signposted. The track rises to a height of 750ft.

Beyond Slattadale the road goes westwards towards the coast where a side road runs down to Red Point via Badachro and Port Henderson. Here, at Redpoint Farm, is the end (or start) of the coast walk to Diabaig. Even if the long walk to Diabaig or Alligin is not contemplated, it is still worthwhile visiting the silvery sands, found both north of Red Point and to the south, near the fishing station. There are superb views to the Cuillin of Skye and the Trotternish coastline.

Gairloch, Inverewe and An Teallach

THE LANDS OF Gairloch were held for a long time by the MacLeods who had a protracted disagreement with the MacKenzies. In 1480 a sister of Hector Roy MacKenzie married Allan, Chief of the Gairloch MacLeods. Allan's brothers despised the two sons of his marriage so much that they murdered him, and then repaired to the island on Loch Tollaidh where his wife was staying with the

◀ *The fishing station near Red Point.*

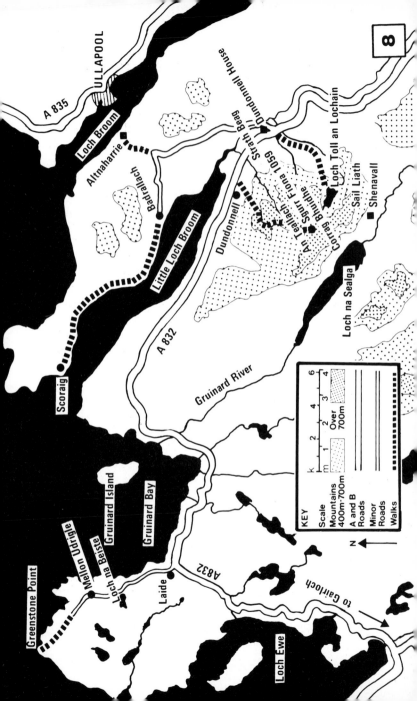

children and killed them as well, throwing the blood-stained shirts at the bereaved mother. She took the shirts as evidence of the dastardly deed to her father, MacKenzie of Seaforth, at Brahan Castle. The old man despatched Hector Roy to the King in Edinburgh and obtained a commission of fire and sword against the MacLeods. In 1494 he was granted the lands of Gairloch by charter from the crown.

Hector Roy's descendants still occupy Flowerdale House, situated amongst the trees on the right just before the road to Gairloch pier is reached. The pier itself is well worth a visit, especially when the boats are landing their catches. It would be difficult to find a more perfect Highland setting. Closer still to Gairloch is a superb bay, guarded by both a graveyard and a golf course. At its westerly end are the ruins of an old fort of the MacLeods of Gairloch, built on the site of an earlier vitrified fort.

Gairloch is a pleasant place to linger. There are ample sandy beaches, though the water may not be as warm as one might expect from its proximity to the Gulf Stream. But the fishing is good. From Melvaig, to the north, a private road leads on to reach Rubha Reidh after four miles. There is an exhilarating walk to the lighthouse. This was the country of Black Findlay of the Arrows, a marksman of olden times.

Inverewe Gardens are situated on Am Ploc Ard (the High Hound Promontory), which used to be a barren spit of land, just like all the others on that rugged coastline round Poolewe. In 1862 only one forlorn willow bush grew there. But Osgood MacKenzie, a man of great drive and imagination, conceived a garden which was to be unique at such a latitude and one which people would come to visit from all over the world. After Osgood's death the care of the garden was

---

Gairloch Harbour and the Torridon peaks. ►

Thursday landings. ► ►

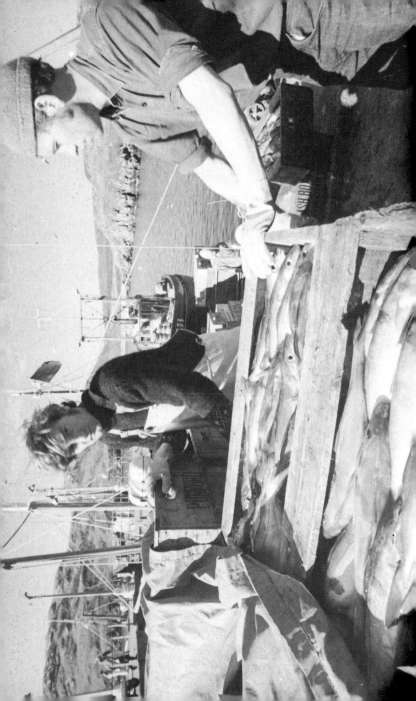

taken over by his daughter who, in 1952, handed it over to the National Trust for Scotland. If you have botanical leanings, you should allow at least one full day – if not two – to view the gardens. The *Magnolia stellata*, seventy-five feet in circumference and twenty-eight feet high, for example, may be the largest specimen in the world. Spring, of course, is the time to visit the gardens, when one is rewarded by a kaleidoscope of colour against a backcloth of the peaks of Flowerdale Forest. There is a licensed restaurant at the entrance to the gardens, also run by the National Trust.

Just before the main road reaches Gruinard Bay, a side turning leads north. Along this, about one mile short of Mellon Udrigle the loch on the left is called Loch na Beiste, the Loch of the Monster. Here yet another cousin of Nessie and Morag used to lurk, finally making an appearance one Sunday long ago, much to the annoyance of the elders en route for the kirk. Incensed at this transgression of the Sabbath, they asked the laird's permission to drain the loch and so get to grips with the creature under more sporting terms. However, this all happened before the advent of mechanical diggers and, the Western Highlands being renowned for relaxing air, a prolonged effort was to no avail. Undaunted, they carried a boat to the loch and ferried out fourteen bags of quicklime which were deposited in the deepest part. The creature never violated another Sabbath!

Mellon Udrigle is a small crofting township found in a perfect setting of close cropped turf, wide sands and green sea; unfortunately it is now largely spoiled by the ubiquitous caravan. The road ends at Mellon Udrigle but it is possible to walk on round to Greenstone Point,

---

◀ *For rest and play. A beach close to Gairloch.*

At Inverewe Gardens with Beinn Airigh Charr in the ▶
distance.

Gruinard Bay and Island from the old church at Laide. ▶ ▶

an excursion which gives extensive views of the island-dotted sea to the north and east, with the Summer Isles and Achiltibuie beyond.

Gruinard Island lies tranquil in Gruinard Bay, apparently just like any other off-shore island. But it was here that the Microbiological Establishment of the Ministry of Defence conducted experiments into the airborne dissemination of anthrax during the last war. Thanks to these experiments an effective vaccine was developed against anthrax, but at the cost of possibly a hundred years contamination of the island which at one time provided good stock grazing. It could be decontaminated – at a cost, and one can't help wondering if the island was situated off the south coast of England whether such measures would not have been taken long ago. Gruinard is a long way from Westminster!

Anyone capable of walking should make the effort to visit the great eastern corrie of An Teallach. No photograph can do it justice. It curves round Loch Toll an Lochain like a cross-cut saw; more often than not skeins of mist cling round its precipices as if a giant smith had recently quenched red hot steel. An Teallach means the Forge and even now, close to the Dundonnell Hotel (famed for its excellent food) there is a small smithy, used as a climbing bothy, which still retains the old bellows and the forge.

The traverse of the peaks of An Teallach is an exhilarating day and one which will be long remembered. It cannot be recommended, however, for the inexperienced hillwalker, as the south buttress of Corrag Bhuidhe has a Bad Step which has been the last step for more than one unfortunate person. But for those with more modest aspirations, the climb to Sgurr Fiona

◄ A waterfall on the path up to Toll an Lochain.

A misty day on the Forge – An Teallach. ►

An Teallach. Corrag Bhuidhe on the left and Sgurr Fiona ► ►
on the right. Toll an Lochain is in the corrie to the right.

(3,474ft/1,059m) – or even on to Corrag Bhuidhe itself – from the Dundonnell side is amply rewarding. The views are exceptional on a good day. A path starts up the hillside close to a cottage half a mile south-east of the hotel; at one point it detours in a long loop but it should be followed all the way to the first summit. The obstacles on the ridge as far as Corrag Bhuidhe can all be avoided on the western side where there is a narrow path. From the cliff edge there is an aerial view of Loch Toll an Lochain. Lord Berkely's Seat is the prominent rock tower between Sgurr Fiona and Corrag Bhuidhe. Corrag Bhuidhe comprises four main towers of Torridonian sandstone and, for all but the experienced, a retreat should be made back along the ridge, retracing the ascent route, for the descent of the Bad Step on the south buttress of Corrag Bhuidhe lies ahead.

Those wishing to visit Toll an Lochain should leave the main road at a point almost opposite Dundonnell House, at a small lay-by close to a stream, and follow the path up through the conifers. The way follows the turbulent Allt Garbh stream as far as a waterfall which cascades into a large pool from the left; then a more direct western line is taken to gain an expanse of boiler plate slabs which, gently inclining, take you to the lochan.

From the lochan it is possible to ascend the left-hand gully (left out of the picture on page 169) and thereby gain the summit of the ridge. Sail Liath can now easily be climbed from the col. On the west side of An Teallach lurks Loch na Sealga (the Loch of the Hunts) whose river, the Gruinard, runs into Gruinard Bay. Part of the long hike from Carnmore to Shenavall can be seen from the An Teallach summit and, to the north, wave upon wave of peaks with magical names call one irresistibly. A return to the main road at Dundonnell House can be made by descending south-east from the summit to the Shenavall-Dundonnell track.

◄ *Crazy sandstone towers, An Teallach.*

Near where this track joins the main road a side road crosses the Dundonnell River and rises above Strath Beag to finish at Badrallach on the north side of Little Loch Broom. Beyond lie the crofts of Scoraig, where latter-day crofters – mainly young people who have vacated the rat race and taken to the soil – have formed a small but industrious community. The walk along the shore path from Badrallach to Scoraig is a pleasant one.

An even easier diversion can be made by walking, from the gate at the high point on the road to Badrallach, across the neck of the peninsula to the Altnaharrie Inn where a ferry operates over to Ullapool (except in bad weather).

From the gentle woods of Strath Beag the road ascends to 1,100ft. This was known as Destitution Road, as it was built during the potato famine of 1851. On a clear day views of An Teallach are obtained during the ascent, its buttresses looking rather like a host of mediaeval castles.

The Corrieshalloch Gorge at Braemore junction was cut by the melt water from a great ice cap, several thousand feet thick, which lay to the south. The Gorge and the 200ft Falls of Measach are in the care of the National Trust for Scotland, and are but a short way from a convenient car park.

▲ ◄ *An Teallach from Toll an Lochain.*
◄ *A crofting scene. Marking lambs.*
The Corrieshalloch Gorge.   ►

Ullapool to Lochinver and the wilds of Assynt

ULLAPOOL IS SITUATED on a late Ice Age beach, fifty feet above sea level. Its Norse name means Ulli's Steading. The present town is comparatively new for this north-western seaboard, having been founded by the British Fisheries Society in 1788, and even today fish play a large part in its economy.

Ullapool is a good centre for exploring the surrounding country, but a car is really essential as some of the walks and climbs are far-flung. In fine weather the many boat trips available offer a unique opportunity to visit some of the islands. All forms of angling are possible here from loch and river fishing to big game fishing for shark and skate. Skate of nearly 200 lbs have been caught.

An enjoyable walk of some twelve miles – which until relatively recent times was made daily by the postman – follows the path from South Keanchulish to Achiltibuie. Branch off left from the A835 four and a half miles north of Ullapool to reach South Kean-chulish; a track leads on from here. After about a mile, turn west to cross the river, and presently a gate in a deer fence gives access to the path which rises to 750ft. From here the track is well marked by cairns, necessary in mist for in places the path is precipitous. Beyond the steep section, at Culnacraig, there are two possible routes: one by Achduart, leading to the Acheninver road, and the other, keeping further inland to Achvraie and Achiltibuie. There is a Youth Hostel at Acheninver.

The easiest route to climb Ben More Coigach (2,438ft/743m) is to leave the road about two and a half miles from the Drumrunie turn off and follow the Allt Claonaidh, then break away from this to gain the east ridge of Coigach. This is straightforward enough and the effort of ascent will be well rewarded, if the day is fine, by a magnificent view. The same route should be used for the return journey.

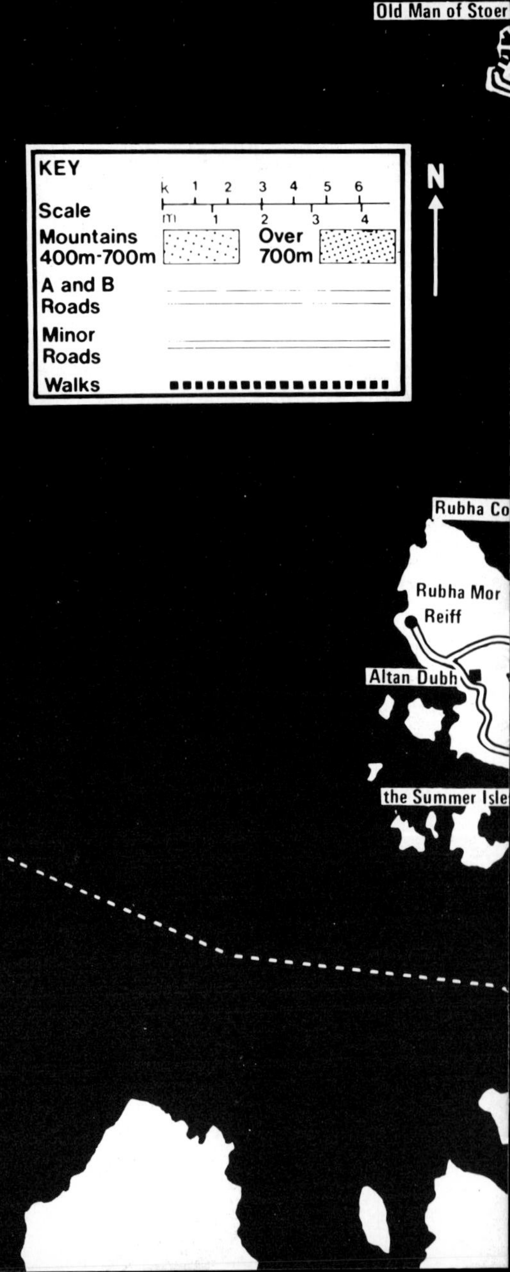
Old Man of Stoer
KEY
Scale
k 1 2 3 4 5 6
m 1 2 3 4
Mountains 400m-700m
Over 700m
A and B Roads
Minor Roads
Walks
N
Rubha Co
Rubha Mor
Reiff
Altan Dubh
the Summer Isle

Inverpolly National Nature Reserve embraces three main peaks: Cul Mor (2,786ft/849m), Cul Beag (2,525ft/769m), and Stac Polly (Pollaidh) (2,009ft/613m). Both Stac Polly and Cul Mor make worthwhile expeditions. Cul Mor can readily be ascended from Knockanrock on the A835. The car park here gives a superb panorama of the peaks and there is a Nature Trail for those wishing to be so organised. But by far the most interesting line of approach to Cul Mor leaves the narrow Achiltibuie road a few hundred yards short of the cottage of Linneraineach where a cairn marks the start of a path. Climb over the bealach and down, taking the right-hand fork of the track to skirt Loch an Doire Dhuibh. Cross the stream to Cul Mor directly above. It is best to head for the lower top of Cul Mor, second from the right and closer to hand. From the summit follow a steep-looking but easy ridge leftwards, with a gully on its left. There are three tops to Cul Mor; the summit, which is of quartzite, lies to the north. In event of cloud (or lack of energy) there is a superb walk round Loch an Doire Dhuibh, following north-west down the bank of the Gleann Laoigh burn to reach a gamekeeper's hut. Ford the stream beyond it, just before reaching Loch Sionascaig, and follow the narrow track back to the junction of paths on the south side of Loch an Doire Dhuibh. Fishing is available on Loch Sionascaig during April, May and June.

There is a fine walk from a point just south of Knockanrock, starting between Lochan Fhada and Clar Loch Beag, to reach the banks of the Gleann Laoigh burn. The stream should be followed to Lochan Gainmheich, and the loch skirted to the right to reach a fisherman's hut. Just beyond this the stream should be

◀ *Loch Kanaird with Ben More Coigach behind.*

Cul Mor, Stac Polly and Cul Beag from Achnahaird. ▶

Stac Polly. The route to the summit is by the low point on ▶ ▶
the ridge.

forded, before Loch Sionascaig, to gain the narrow track which should be taken back to the path junction, then on to Linneraineach.

Stac Polly is a mountain straight out of a fairy tale. Its contorted sandstone pinnacles and castellated profile are a delight to view, especially from the summit ridge of the mountain, and the traverse of this ridge is not exacting provided you have a reasonable head for heights. From the car park on Loch Lurgainn, just to the south of the peak, a path runs up to the saddle, left of the eastern summit. Once on top, head right for the ascent of the eastern buttress and left for the western, which takes you along the serrated edge, giving one of the finest prospects in the area. The obstacles en route can easily be avoided if you follow the prints of countless feet. The western buttress itself offers unrestricted views out over the Atlantic. Northwards the great bulk of Suilven dominates the landscape, whilst to its right Cul Mor rises above its watery doorstep. To the south, across Loch Lurgainn, is Ben More Coigach and its satellites; Sgurr an Fhidhleir looks especially elegant. Return back along the ridge and you'll be amazed at what you have missed travelling westwards, as new vistas unfold before you.

A visit to the sandstone peninsula of Rubha Mor (by road) is worthwhile. The road continues past Stac Polly along the northern shores of the interlinked lochs – Lurgainn, Bad a' Ghaill and Osgaig. A left-hand fork in the road beyond this last loch takes you to the crofts of Altan Dubh, a delightful community, whilst a further branch continues northwards up the

---

◄ *Southwards from the summit ridge of Stac Polly with Beinn an Eoin on the left beyond Loch Lurgainn and Sgurr an Fhidhleir beyond the small Lochan Dearg.*

The sandstone pinnacles of Stac Polly. ►

The south face of Cul Mor from the east end of Stac Polly. ► ►

coast a short way to Reiff. Here, ruins tell the old story of migration and lack of work. Continuing on foot beyond these dwellings gives access to a superb sandy bay; from here the coast line – all the way to Rubha Coigeach – offers almost a surfeit of delightful views.

There is a salmon fishery just north of Achiltibuie, where it is possible to hire boats in which to visit the Summer Isles and other islands further off-shore.

In its wild way Assynt is one of the most appealing regions of Scotland. Here is the Scotland that people who have never visited the country visualise: naked rocks, like the aftermath of an atomic holocaust, litter the moorland; the mass of Suilven, as seen from Lochinver, is upraised like a huge monument amid a thousand lochans. The Vikings called the area Sudrland, the South Land, and added it to their kingdom of Orkney and Shetland when they overran the region in the eleventh century. It was over a hundred years before William the Lion, King of Scots, won it back. Entering Assynt on the tortuous road from Badnagyle makes one realise why young Lochinvar needed such a good horse!

> O, young Lochinvar is come out of the west,
> Through all the wide Border his steed was the best:
> And save his good broadsword he weapons had none,
> He rode all unarm'd, and he rode all alone.
> So faithful in love, and so dauntless in war,
> There never was knight like the young Lochinvar.

Lochinver provides the essentials for those who like open spaces, the hills, and loch and sea fishing. It is a

◄ *Stac Polly on the left and Cul Beag from Loch Bad a'Ghaill.*

Looking over Altan Dubh to the Summer Isles with Skye ►
beyond.

Lochinver and Suilven. ► ►

busy fishing port, with large annual catches of white fish. Behind the village – basically one street only – stretches the expanse of the Glencanisp Forest, a gneiss wilderness, at one time covered by forest, since burned – probably by the Vikings – and now a deer forest.

Suilven is one of the most striking peaks on the Scottish mainland. Its western sentinel, Caisteal Liath (2,399ft/731m), dominates Lochinver. Seated on an 800ft plateau of gneiss, the mountain is sandstone, capped with grey (*liath*) quartzite. The ascent of Suilven provides a long day and, except for the rock climber – for whom there are a variety of routes directly up the western flank of Caisteal Liath –the low point of Bealach Mor, south-east of Caisteal Liath, is the best means of ascent. The summit ridge can be reached from either north or south at this point. There is a choice of routes to gain the lower defences of the mountain. From Lochinver you can take the narrow road to Glencanisp Lodge, beyond which a stalker's path leads on to Suileag. Here the path from Little Loch Assynt is joined, the latter provides an alternative route from the north, starting from the bridge at the western extremity of Loch Assynt. From Suileag the path is followed to Lochan Buidhe where you must head south to reach the lochans immediately below the mountain. Bealach Mor is above and an obvious gully ahead provides the link to the top. The summit of Caisteal Liath is reached by going north-west from the bealach. En route for the summit, a drystone dyke is encountered, cresting the summit ridge; this was reputedly built to prevent sheep straying on to the steep flanks of "the Castle". The other peaks of the Suilven ridge should only be attempted by

◄ *Suilven, Caisteal Liath from Lochinver.*

Meall Mheadhonach from Caisteal Liath. ►

Looking towards the "New World" from an abandoned croft house north of Lochinver. ► ►

experienced hill walkers with a basic knowledge of climbing.

A different route in to Suilven starts from Inverkirkaig, a few miles to the south of Lochinver. The River Kirkaig should be followed past the turbulent Falls of Kirkaig to Fionn Loch. At the west end of the loch (it is sometimes possible to hire a boat, saving a long hike) take a slanting, rising line to gain the slopes below Bealach Mor on the southern side. It should be stressed that the ascent of Caisteal Liath should only be attempted by those who are fit and who have experience in hill walking. In event of high wind or bad weather, one of the many lower excursions should be made instead.

A walk of thirteen miles can be made from Lochinver past Glencanisp Lodge to Elphin; though rather wet in places, the expedition takes one through the heart of Assynt. The path continues beyond the Lodge (as described for the northerly approach route up Suilven) to cross the stream beyond Lochan Buidhe and follows the north-east shore of Loch na Gainimh, then the southerly shore of Lochan Fhada. At this point the path is not very obvious. Close to Loch a' Chroisg turn south to gain Cam Loch. The south-east shoreline (somewhat damp) should be followed closely, to reach the main road near Elphin. Before the construction of the Inchnadamph–Lochinver road, this route was in regular use.

An alternative walk can be made by heading north at Suileag to gain the Inchnadamph–Lochinver road at Little Assynt.

Loch Assynt to Nedd offers a fine walk in the shadow of the great southerly cliffs of Quinag. The walk begins

◄ *Feeding red deer.*

Suilven from Elphin, showing the southerly aspect of ►
Bealach Mor above the left chimney.

Cul Mor and Suilven from the graveyard at Elphin. ► ►

at Tumore; behind the cottage a path rises up the hill in an easy gradient to Bealach Leireag. From here the route follows the northern side of the glen and of Loch an Leothaid, to reach the road close to Nedd.

The territory to the south of Nedd and Drumbeg is a "vacant lot" or rock and loch but, further west, the Point of Stoer is well worth attention, even if it is only to visit the Old Man, a craggy rock plinth of Torridonian sandstone which has for centuries endured the ravages of the Atlantic. The stack is ascended regularly by rock climbers who rate it Hard Severe. You can either set off from close by the lighthouse on the west of the peninsula and traverse the tops of the cliffs up the coast past the Old Man to reach the Point, or start from Culkein, to the south-east of the Point, and follow the rough track used by crofters to transport their peat, past Loch Cul Fraioch. By taking the right fork beyond the loch, peat hags will be reached. If you cross these on the left, the top of Sidhean Mor can be climbed without undue effort. The panorama from here is quite breathtaking. To reach the Old Man from the top you should descend northwards. This whole stretch of coastline merits exploration as it is the haunt of countless seabirds, whilst the rock architecture, enhanced by the sea, is definitely worth viewing. The somewhat featureless hinterland of the Stoer peninsula provides an extensive peat supply for local crofters.

Quinag (the Gaelic *cuinneag* means a milk stoup)

◄ *Suilven from the road to Nedd. Access to Bealach Mor from the north is to the left of Caisteal Liath, the peak in the foreground.*

Loch Assynt Lodge with Quinag behind. The cottage of ► *Tumore is to the right on the main road.*

On the path from Tumore to Nedd, Assynt, at the Bealach ► ► *Leireag. Above is the great westerly cliff of Quinag. Access to the summit ridge of Quinag can be gained by a bealach just right of the photograph.*

towers 2,653ft (808m) above Loch Assynt. There are seven tops in all, forming a giant Y. Facing Kylesku ferry, the northerly ramparts of Sail Ghorm boasts several rock climbs, mainly on the prominent Barrel Buttress, clearly seen from the main road, or from the switchback Kylesku–Drumbeg road. The ascent of the peaks of Quinag presents no difficulty if tackled from about two miles up the Kylesku road from Skiag Bridge on the north shore of Loch Assynt. Here the slopes of Spidean Coinich can be followed to its summit and the other tops thereby gained. Alternatively it is possible to make the ascent from the Bealach Leireag by breaching the great western ramparts of the cliffs at the low point of the ridge above it. To take in all the tops represents a fairly strenuous day, but a memorable one.

A hero's betrayal and the Inchnadamph caves

BETWEEN INCHNADAMPH AND Skiag Bridge stand the ruins of Ardvreck Castle. Its history is linked with the betrayal and death of James Graham, the Marquis of Montrose, a gifted general and the greatest Scotsman of his time.

Montrose was abroad when he heard of the execution of his King, Charles I, in 1649. He felt compelled to take up arms against the insurgent Convenanters and with permission from Charles II – then in exile – he sailed for the Orkneys the following year. Unfortunately his courageous bid shared the same fate as many other invading forces on Scotland's shores: many of his supply ships were wrecked in storms, so that when he landed in Caithness he had only forty horses, 400

◄ *The Torridonian sandstone pinnacle of the Old Man of Stoer, Assynt.*

The road to Nedd and Kylesku from Lochinver. ►

Loch Nedd with Quinag behind. ► ►

Danes, and 1,000 untrained troops. Montrose had expected the support of MacKenzie, Earl of Seaforth, and his powerful clan, but MacKenzie had heard word that Charles II, unbeknown to Montrose was trying to make a deal with the Government, so he withheld his support.

Despite this, Montrose marched south and was defeated at Invershin by Colonel Strachan who, although his army was smaller, had 220 trained and mounted dragoons. Montrose was in dire straits. He had his horse shot and went over the pass from Strath Oykell into Assynt, asking for food and shelter at Ardvreck, since the MacLeods of Assynt were reputedly followers of Charles II. The chief at that time was the unscrupulous twenty-two-year-old Neil MacLeod, eleventh chief. Knowing there was a £25,000 reward on Montrose's head, he sent word to General Leslie at Tain that he had Montrose in his dungeons. Montrose, a sick man, was bound to a horse and taken to Edinburgh where he was hanged in the Grassmarket.

Neil MacLeod's act was contrary to all Highland traditions of honour. A century later Charles Edward Stewart, with £30,000 on his head, was betrayed by no one in the breadth of the Highlands. Neil took his ill-gotten gain, £20,000 Scots; the rest was made up with 400 bolls of meal which turned out to be rotten. From then on the fortunes of the MacLeods declined. MacKenzie of Seaforth raided Assynt, causing a wave of destruction and carrying off over 2,000 cattle, 1,500 horses and 6,000 sheep and goats. Strangely, he smashed containers holding 50,000 merks worth of brandy and wine which were on a ship anchored off the coast.

When Charles II came to the throne, Neil was pronounced a rebel. Letters of Fire and Sword were issued

---

◀ *Looking back to Sail Gharbh, Quinag, from near Kylesku.*

and MacKenzie took over Assynt, holding it for a century. (Neil is supposed to have escaped to Holland). It was bought from the MacKenzies in 1760 by the Earl of Sutherland, the family who, 600 years before, had gifted the lands to the MacNicols of Ullapool for assistance in fighting the Viking invaders.

Close to Ardvreck are the ruins of Calda House, built by the MacKenzies when they took over the estate. It was allegedly burned by the MacRaes of Kintail who had made a vow that no Earl of Sutherland should occupy it. Assynt suffered heavily later, during the Clearances, and many of the inhabitants were shipped to the Colonies.

Inchnadamph – the stag's meadow – is famous for its caves which occur in the Cambrian limestone belt. It is a much harder limestone than the Carboniferous, but nevertheless the caves attract the attention of spelaeologists and the area is of great geological and botanical interest. There are caves near both the Traligill and Allt nan Uamh burns; those by the latter stream were excavated in 1917 and two human skeletons were found, of the Azilian period (6,000 BC) besides the bones of northern lynx and bear. The Traligill burn, behind Inchnadamph, goes underground for 350 yards.

The Hotel Inchnadamph provides a good centre for exploring the area. Ben More Assynt (3,273ft/998m) is a prodigious mass of gneiss crowned with snowy quartzite. Up Gleann Dubh, the lower western slopes are of limestone which outcrops all along the Moine Thrust plane. The whole region from Knockan up to Kylesku

◄ *Ardvreck Castle, Loch Assynt.*

Montrose was held in the dungeon at Ardvreck Castle, ►
before being taken to Edinburgh to be hanged. In the
background is the Quinag.

Eas a'Chual Aluinn, Assynt. This is the highest waterfall ► ►
in Britain. The vertical drop is 658 feet.

forms a geological boundary, Archaean gneiss to the west, Moine Schist to the east. The latter moved along the slide plane from the north and east to envelop the gneiss.

As one passes over the high ground on the A894 between Loch Assynt and Kylesku ferry, two paths lead eastwards, one either side of Loch na Gainmhich, to join and continue to Loch Bealach a' Bhuirich (1,600ft/487m), before descending to the waterfall of Eas a' Chual Aluinn, the Splendid Waterfall of Coul, where the vertical drop is 658ft. There are two paths down past the waterfall, one either side; the righthand one probably leads to the best viewpoint, well back from the bottom. Unfortunately, the falls can be disappointing during dry weather; certainly nothing like their rival, the Falls of Glomach, further south.

Arkle, the Great Stack of Handa and Sandwood Bay

THE SHORT CROSSING from Kylesku is served by a ferry which, until recent times, was free. Alas, no more. Close to the jetty on the southern side an hotel is situated amidst grandiose scenery. To the east of the ferry the water divides into two lochs: Glencoul and Glendhu. The point thus formed, Aird da Loch, is of great geological interest, showing an exposure of the Glencoul Thrust plane. The Stack of Glencoul stands at the far end of Loch Glencoul. Westwards, beyond the narrows, is Loch a' Chairn Bhain which washes out into the Atlantic through Eddrachillis Bay.

From Kylestrome one enters the Reay Forest, a wild tract of country with few roads, few people, but plenty of exposed rock and lochans; studying a map, or the terrain itself from one of its stark hills, one wonders where all this water originates. The hills in the forest

Kylesku ferry.

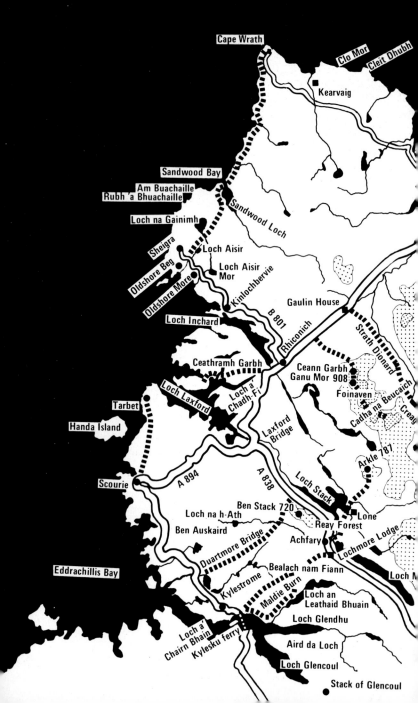

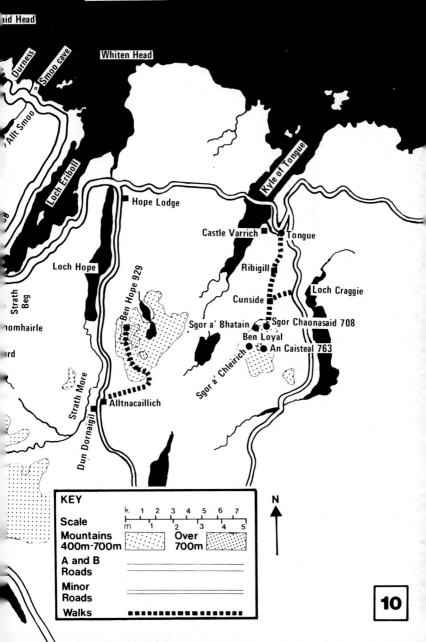

PENTLAND FIRTH

aid Head

Durness
Whiten Head
Smoo cave
Allt Smoo

Loch Eriboll

Kyle of Tongue

Hope Lodge

Castle Varrich
Tongue

Loch Hope

Ribigill

Strath Beg

Ben Hope 929

Loch Craggie

Cunside

nomhairle

Sgor a' Bhatain
Sgor Chaonasaid 708

rd

Ben Loyal
An Caisteal 763

Strath More

Sgor a' Chleirich

Alltnacaillich

Dun Dornaigil

KEY

Scale

k 1 2 3 4 5 6 7

m   1   2   3   4   5

Mountains
400m-700m

Over
700m

A and B
Roads

Minor
Roads

Walks

N

10

are of Cambrian quartzite, which, to the south of Glen-coul, had only been apparent on the summits. Here it lies on top of the gneiss, with the exception of a few places such as Handa and Cape Wrath.

This was the land of the Clan MacKay. In 1829 Lord Reay sold the property to George Leveson-Gower, a man detested by the Highlanders. He evicted 15,000 men, women and children from their homes; homes which were subsequently burned to make way for the new god – sheep. Alas, they did not produce the golden fleeces he had hoped for, such is the way of State and bureaucracy, but he was created a duke – Duke of Sutherland. One of the Duke's better deeds was the construction of the road north from the ferry, cut through stubborn gneiss at a cost of £40,000. This tortuous road is the one still in use today.

From the north side of Kylesku ferry a track leads to the A838 at Loch More. It follows the shore of Loch Glendhu and branches off at the Maldie Burn, taking the western bank of this burn past an impressive water-fall. It then climbs above Loch an Leathaid Bhuain where it joins another track which has the same start-ing point on the north side of the ferry; this path can be followed back to make a circular walk from Kyle-strome. The route on to Loch More continues via the Bealach nam Fiann, then eastwards downhill to Lochmore Lodge.

Achfary, just a mile up the road, offers the best approach to Arkle (2,580ft/787m). Take the track round the south-east end of Loch Stack to the bothy at Lone. From here the path continues north-east and gives access to the main ridge. It is possible to continue on the ridge all the way (four miles) to Foinaven, but it is preferable to ascend this latter peak from Rhiconich.

About three and a half miles out from Kylesku on the Scourie road a further track bites into the hills and wasteland to the north-east from Duartmore Bridge, to

◄ *The islands of Eddrachillis Bay.*

reach Loch Stack after nine miles. It keeps to the south-east of Ben Auskaird and to the south-east side of Loch na h-Ath, skirting the north-western slopes of Ben Stack to gain the A838. Ben Stack itself can be climbed from this side, a steep, but relatively straightforward climb. Being 2,364ft (720m) high and fairly isolated, it offers wide unobstructed views from its summit.

Scourie is situated nine miles north of Kylestrome in a sheltered hollow by the sea. Two miles to the north-west is the island of Handa, a bird sanctuary under the Royal Society for the Protection of Birds. Handa is no longer inhabited, though in 1843 twelve families lived there. It can be reached by boat from either Scourie or Tarbet, further up the coast; there is a footpath from Scourie to Tarbet. At one time the island was ruled by a queen and parliament, like the island of St. Kilda. Parliament met each morning to discuss daily problems, presided over by the queen who was the oldest widow on the island. Like the St. Kildans, the Handa people lived largely on birds, for the island has a wealth of guillemots, fulmars, puffins and razorbills. The bird diet was supplemented by potatoes and fish, and it was the great potato famine of 1848 which forced the population to move to America.

Handa is well worth visiting, even if you are not a bird lover. The whole island has a fairytale quality and, appropriately, the highest point (at 406ft) is named Sithean Mor, the Great Hill of the Fairies. At the northern end great sandstone cliffs rise a sheer 350ft out of the sea. The graveyard close to the landing beach was used by people from the mainland as well as the islanders, for the Reay Forest was at one time plagued by wolves.

◄ *Scourie.*

Guardians of Handa. ►

Climbers on the first ascent of the Great Stack of Handa. ► ►

The Great Stack of Handa is the dominating feature of the island. Squatting on its five legs, it snuggles into its parent island, separated by only the narrowest of channels, as if to shelter from the savage Atlantic. At its nearest point to the main island, on the west side, the gap is a mere 80 ft. An "ascent" of the Stack was made as long ago as 1876, when a stalwart bunch of Lewismen came to Handa to collect eggs and birds. One of them, Donald MacDonald, succeeded in reaching the top of the Stack, not by climbing, however, but with the aid of his companions who took a long rope, approximately 500ft, round the bay in which the Stack is enclosed, anchoring and tensioning it so that it lay taut across the top. He then crossed over, hand over hand. Once on the summit, he drove in stakes (which were visible until recent times) and rigged up a breeches buoy so that his companions could join him. In modern times this feat has been emulated, with the aid of climbing safety equipment. The Stack has also been climbed from the sea on the north-west side, starting from a boat. The route is of Very Severe standard. The late Alasdair Monro of Tarbet, a daring and competent seaman, took a small wooden boat under the Stack, between its legs. He also took his boat through the tunnel which links the north end of the channel of the Stack to the precipitous geo to the west. Circumnavigating the Stack is a fascinating and awe-inspiring experience. Above, birds line the 350ft rock galleries, reminding one of the interior of a great opera house, the patrons dressed for a gala performance. At intervals a bore comes through the channel providing a few anxious moments.

The bays and inlets of this northern coast were the playground of the Vikings. Today, all that remain to mark their occupation of this territory are the names. All the five large sea lochs which bite into this hard

---

◄ *The Great Stack of Handa. The gap on the left was the one crossed by rope by the Lewismen in 1876.*

shoreline have Norse names: Tongue, from Tunga, Tongue of land; Eriboll, from Eyrr bol, Beach Town; Durness, Point of the Wild Beast; Inchard, from Engi-ford or Meadow Loch; and Laxford, the Salmon Loch – for which it is still famous today.

Laxford Bridge is important for its road junction, but little else. From here the road runs across the spine of Scotland, following the convenient valleys by Loch More and Loch Shin and providing an important link with the east coast.

Before reaching Rhiconich, the wild region of Ceath-ramh Garbh (well-named "Rough Quarter") lies to the west. A road leading into it from a point about three quarters of a mile south-west of Rhiconich enables part of its rugged coastline to be explored from the north shore of Loch a' Chadh-Fi. At Rhiconich the main road heads north-east towards Durness, but a left-hand branch follows the edge of Loch Inchard – very similar to a Norwegian fjord – with the prodigious mass of Foinaven rising directly behind Rhiconich.

Kinlochbervie is famous for its white fish landings. There are two jetties, one each side of the peaceful isthmus; peaceful, at least until a Thursday afternoon when the boats come in with their escort of screaming gulls. One is now almost running out of road in these far reaches of Scotland; in fact, the road finishes at Sheigra, four miles north-west of Kinlochbervie, after passing close by the crofting communities of Oldshore More and Oldshore Beg. Oldshore More is an unfor-gettable place, exuding an aura of tranquillity; the sands below the village are some of the finest within easy access of a road and, as usual, are overlooked by a graveyard. In 1263 King Hakon rounded Cape Wrath

◄ *Ben Stack from near Laxford Bridge.*

Foinaven, Arkle and Ben Stack beyond Loch Inchard ►
from the road to Kinlochbervie.

The sands at Oldshore More as seen from the road. ► ►

with his Viking fleet of a hundred ships and anchored here at the start of his invasion of the Scottish mainland.

An even finer beach than Oldshore More is that of Sandwood Bay, a few miles to the north. They are miles that you must walk, but the reward more than justifies the effort, for here is a beach fashioned in a grand scale, more magnificent than any other I have ever seen, even in the Southern Hemisphere. Great breakers wash it, impeded by no land to the west until Greenland. Behind the beach a wide band of marram grass dunes separates it from the freshwater Sandwood Loch. A derelict, reputedly haunted house overlooks the loch. The path to the beach leaves the road about half a mile past the Oldshore More turn-off and passes Loch Aisir and several other lochs before dipping down to the beach after four miles of easy going. To the west of the beach, off the Rubh'a Bhuachaille, is Am Buachaille, a pillar of sandstone standing in the water.

◄ *A "rock garden", Oldshore More.*
Oldshore More. ►
Sandwood Bay, Sutherland. ► ►

Foinaven, Cape Wrath and Ben Loyal

FOINAVEN IS BEST approached, by those intent on climbing it, from the Durness road, about three miles north-east of Rhiconich. Like its neighbour, Arkle, it is composed of quartzite, lending it a snowy appearance from afar. At 2,980ft (908m), Ganu Mor is the highest top of the range. Leave the road just north of Lochan Cul na Creige. The ground can be boggy after wet weather, but a route towards the first top can be found without encountering any difficulty. The top of Ceann Garbh (2,952ft/900m) is reached first, followed by Ganu Mor. For those feeling fit it is possible to continue on to Creag Urbhard over the pass of Cadha na Beucaich. The cliffs of Creag Urbhard are the haunt of both eagles and rock climbers. Needless to say, this expedition makes a long day and should only be undertaken by the fit, blessed also with good weather. You should return by the same route.

The wide open Strath Dionard leads down into Durness. Here the country is more lush and open. To the north and west lies Cape Wrath, out of sight over the intervening Moor of Parph. It is not possible to drive across the Kyles of Durness to enter this region, but you can take the ferry from Keoldale; on the far side a minibus service is operated to Cape Wrath. The difficulty in reaching this remote part of the British Isles is worth the effort involved. To the right, on the way to the lighthouse, are the highest sea-cliffs on the British mainland, the Cleit Dhubh, 850ft and, further to the north, the Clo Mor, 600ft. Beyond the Clo Mor is the delectable cove of Kearvaig.

Cape Wrath lighthouse is perched 370ft above the sea and its light can be seen for twenty-seven miles. The

◄ The ferry across the Kyles of Durness to the Cape Wrath. road.
A natural arch near Cape Wrath. ►
The 600 foot cliffs of Clo Mor, Cape Wrath. ► ►

cliffs round the lighthouse were at one time the home of the sea eagle, now long vanished from these Scottish cliffs, but being re-introduced further south on the Island of Rhum. The name Cape Wrath is derived from the Norse *Hvarf*, "a turning point". From here there is no more land northwards to the North Pole.

Durness is a happy little village sitting astride limestone cliffs. The coast is indented by sandy bays, the most famous of which, a mile to the west, is Balnakeil, meaning "Place of the Kirk". At the southern end of this fine mile and a half stretch of sand is the ruined church of Balnakeil, at one time under the jurisdiction of Dornoch Abbey. Robb Donn, the famous Gaelic poet, was buried by the old kirk in 1777. You can walk along the beach to reach a path to Faraid Head where there are huge marram dunes.

On the road to Loch Eriboll (called Loch 'Orrible by military personnel stationed there during the war), some two miles from Durness, is found the Smoo Cave, the name is probably derived from "Smuga", the Norse for "a cleft". The Allt Smoo drops eighty feet down a vertical hole, exposes itself again in a cavern, before exiting through a gorge. The cave can be inspected by descending a steep path and crossing the Allt Smoo to reach the outer cave through a fifty-foot high arch. To gain the inner cave, re-cross the river and ascend to a ledge in order to look over a barrier of rock. The eighty-foot waterfall hides out of view at the end of a twenty-five yard passageway. To the right of the waterfall is another cave system which has many stalagmites and penetrates a further hundred feet, but these innermost recesses are best left to spelaeologists.

Loch Eriboll is the sole breeding ground on the mainland of the Atlantic grey seal; the seals make use of the many caves. The eastern shore of the loch

▲ ◄ *Cape Wrath.*

◄ *Balnakeil Bay, Durness, from the old church built in 1619.*

extends to Whiten Head; this headland was formerly known as Kennagall, "the Headland of the Strangers", which no doubt referred to the Vikings. Where Loch Eriboll mingles with the Pentland Firth, the 500ft high cliffs of Whiten Head demark the extremity of the Moine Thrust Plane. Indeed, the name derives from the area; the desolate peat-moss region between the road to Tongue and the nose of the peninsula is called a'Mhoine.

From the head of Loch Eriboll it is possible to reach Loch Dionard and the base of the great cliffs of Creag Urbhard and Foinaven. A rough track leaves the main road at the head of the loch and cuts through Strath Beg (damp under foot) to the cottage of Strathbeg. It then continues, passing below Shomhairle, and by the bealach over the ridge to Loch Dionard. It is feasible to return via Strath Dionard to Gualin House on the Rhiconich-Durness road. But this involves a considerable distance and there is the added difficulty of transport at the far end, should you have to return and pick up your vehicle from Loch Eriboll.

There are two other mountains worth attention in the area: Ben Hope (3,050ft/929m), and Ben Loyal (2,504ft/763m). The best view of Ben Hope is from Hope Lodge, sixteen miles from Tongue. The mountain's north-western slopes can be seen falling steeply to Strath More. On this side are two obvious terraces with about 1,000ft between them. Above the upper terrace the face is riven with gullies and rock walls. From Hope Lodge a narrow road runs down to Altnaharra; the ascent route for Ben Hope starts at Alltnacaillich. Opposite the large farm building, a path

---

▲ ◄ *The Smoo Cave, Durness.*
◄ *Loch Eriboll.*
Whiten Head from the main road south-east of Durness. ►
At the head of Loch Eriboll. A route to Creag Urbhard, ► ►
Foinaven, leaves the main road and takes a track for a short way, following beneath the cliffs in the background.

follows the burn, steeply at first. Where it levels off, cross over to gain the easy cairned southern ridge of Ben Hope and follow it to the top. Near the road, beyond Alltnacaillich, is the Dun Dornaigil broch, a fine example of its kind. It is twenty-seven feet in diameter within; the walls are fourteen feet thick. Of particular interest is the large triangular lintel. Close to here is the reputed birthplace of Robb Donn, the Gaelic poet who is buried at the churchyard at Balnakeil.

Castle Varrich, to the west of Tongue, was once a MacKay stronghold. The Gaelic name for Tongue was Geann-t-Saile A'Mhicaoidh, "the Head of MacKay's Salt Water". To the north of the village is Tongue House, constructed in 1678 by the Chief of MacKay, Lord Reay.

Ben Loyal, lying to the south of the Kyle of Tongue, is sometimes called the Queen of Scottish Peaks. It is certainly a graceful mountain, as one imagines a queen should be. The finest view is from the north where the four granite peaks of the massif are seen to greatest advantage. Probably the best line for an ascent is to take the Durness road to the Ribigill turn-off. A track leads past the cottage at Cunside where steep grass slopes rise from the east to Sgor Chaonasaid (2,320ft/708m), the most northerly peak of the ridge: the cliffs to the north of the peak should be avoided. An alternative line of ascent is from the road by Loch Craggie. A mile south of Sgor Chaonasaid is An Caisteal (2,504ft/763m), the highest point on the mountain, with a series of steep drops on its south side. Between these two peaks are the two tops of Sgor a'Bhatain. The peak, Sgor a' Chleirich (2,100ft/640m), which lies to the west of An Caisteal, provides the best rock climbing on the mountain with a crag of over 800ft. The descent can be made from the summit of An Caisteal to the roadside at Loch Loyal at almost any point.

◄ *Ben Hope from Hope Lodge.*
The broch at Ben Hope.
Lochan Hacoin and Ben Loyal.

► ►►

Gaelic and Norse Glossary

A	river, stream; terminally: -a, e.g. Calda (*kalda*), cold stream; gen: ar, e.g. Aros (*ar-oss*), river's mouth. (Norse).
Aber, Abar,	also as: Obar, mouth or confluence of a river.
Abhainn, Amhainn	usually Avon, river.
Achadh	usually Ach, field, park.
Ailean	a green place; plain.
Airidh	sheiling.
Aisir	a rocky defile or pass.
Allt	also as: Ald, Alt, Auld, Ault, burn, brook, stream.
Aoineadh	a steep promontory or brae.
Aonach	a height, a ridge.
Ard, Aird	a high point, promontory.
Ath	a ford, also a kiln.
Ay, Ey, I	island, e.g. Pabbay, priest's island; Rona, rough island; Handa, sand island (Norse).
Baile	usually Bal, Bali, town, homestead.
Bàn	white, fair.
Bàrr	a point, extremity.
Bàrd	a poet, a dyke, enclosure, ward.
Beag	also as: Beg, little, small.
Bealach	breach, pass, gap, col.
Beinn	also as: Ben, a mountain.
Beithe	a birch tree.
Bian	a hide (of cattle).
Bidean	summit, e.g. Bidean Druim nan Ramh, summit of the ridge of oars.
Binnean	also as: Binnein, a pinnacle or little mountain.
Blàr	a plain, battlefield.
Bò (pl. Bà)	cow, cows.
Bodach	an old man, hobgoblin, spectre.
Ból	farm, abode, e.g. Ullapool, Ulli's farm; Resipol. (Norse).
Borg	fort, e.g. Boreraig, fort bay. (Norse).
Bost	township, e.g. Kirkabost, church town.(Norse).
Both	also as: Bothan, a hut, booth or bothy.
Bràigh	usually Brae, Bread, top, summit.
Brekka	a slope, e.g. Clibrick, cliff. (Norse).
Bròg	a shoe.
Bruaich	a bank, brae, brim, steep place.
Buachaille	a herdsman.
Buidhe	yellow, golden coloured.
Cadh	a pass, steep path.
Cailleach	a nun, old woman, a witch.
Caisteal	castle, e.g. Caisteal Uisdean, Hugh's castle.
Cam	crooked, bent, one-eyed.
Camas	also as: Camus, bay, bend, channel.
Caol	also as: Caolas, Kyle, strait, firth, narrow.
Càrn	a heap of stones, cairn.
Carr	broken ground.
Ceann	also as: Ken, Kin, head, headland, e.g. Ceann na Beinn, head of the mountain.

Cill, Kil   a cell, church.
Cioch   a pap, woman's breast, e.g. Sgurr na Ciche, peak of the pap.
Clach   a stone.
Clachan   stones, hamlet.
Cladh   a churchyard, a burying place.
Clais   a hollow.
Cleit   a ridge, reef; rocky eminence.
Cnap   a knob, hillock.
Cnoc, Knock a knoll.
Coill, Coille a wood, forest.
Coire   Anglicised form: Corrie, a cauldron, kettle, circular hollow.
Corran   a sickle; semi-circular bay.
Creag   also as: Craig, a rock, cliff, e.g. Creag an Iolaire, eagle's rock.
Crioch   boundary, frontier, landmark.
Crò   a sheep-fold, pen.
Crom   bent, sloping, crooked.
Cruach   stack, heap, haunch.
Cuinneag   a milking pail or stoup, e.g. Quinag, from its shape.
Cùl   the back.
Ciùe   nook.

Dail   a field. Cf. Dalr, e.g. Armadale, bay dale; Bracadale, slope dale; Arnisdale, Arni's dale. (Norse).
Dearg   red.
Doire   grove, hollow.
Druim   also as: Drem, Drom, Drum, the back, ridge.
Dobhar   water, a stream, e.g. Morar, great water.
Dorus   door. Deoch an doruis, a stirrup-cup.
Dubh, Dhu black, dark.
Dùn   a fort, castle, heap.

Eagach   notched.
Eala   a swan.
Ear   east.
Eas   a waterfall.
Easach   a cascade.
Easg   bog, fen, natural ditch.
Eilean   an island.
Eyrr   gravelly bank or beach, e.g. Erradale, gravel beach dale.

Fada   long. e.g. Beinn Fhada, long mountain.
Fas, Fasadh a stance, a firm spot, e.g. Fassiefern, the alder stance.
Feadan   narrow glen.
Fearn   an alder tree.
Féith   bog, sinewy stream, a vein.
Fiadh   a deer.
Fionn   fair, white, e.g. Fionaven, the White Ben.
Fjall   hill, fell, e.g. Helaval, flagstone fell. (Norse).
Fjord   firth, e.g. Snizort, Sni's firth or snow firth; Ainort, Einor's firth; Sunart (Suaineort), Svein's bay. (Norse).
Fuaran   a perennial spring, well.

Gabhar   a goat.

Garbh, Garve	rough, e.g. Garbh Bheinn, rough, wild mountain.
Geal	white, clear, bright.
Geodha	a narrow creek, chasm, rift, cove.
Gearanach	a wall-like ridge.
Geàrr	short.
Gil	cleft, e.g. Idrigil, outer cleft. (Norse).
Glais	a stream, burn.
Glas	grey, pale, wan, green.
Glac	a hollow, dell, defile.
Gleann	usually Glen, narrow valley, dale, dell.
Gob	point, beak.
Gorm	blue, azure, green.
Gualann	shoulder of mountain or hill.
Inbhir	also as: Inver, confluence of river and sea.
Iubhair	yew tree.
Lag	usually Lagan, Logie, a hollow in a hill.
Lair	an axe.
Lairig	the sloping face of a hill, a pass.
Leac	a ledge, e.g. Leac na Fionn, the bright ledge.
Leathad	a slope, declivity.
Leathan	broad.
Leitir	a slope.
Liath	grey.
Linne	pool, sound, channel.
Lòn	a marsh, morass.
Lùb	a bend, fold, curvature.
Màm	a round or gently rising hill.
Maol	headland, bald top, cape.
Meall	knob, lump, rounded hill.
Monadh	moor, heath, hill, mountain.
Mòine	also as: Mointeach, peat-mossland, mossy
Mór	great, large, tall. Anglicised form: More.
Muc	a pig, e.g. Eilean nam Muc, Isle of Muck.
Muileann	mill.
Muir	the sea.
Mullach	a rounded hill.
Nes	nose, point, promontory, e.g. Waternish, water ness; Duirinish, deer ness; Greshornish, pig ness. (Norse).
Odhar	dapple, drab, dun-coloured, sallow.
Ord	a round, steep, or conical hill.
Os	outlet of a lake or river. C.f. Oss, river mouth. (Norse).
Pit, Pet	farm, hollow.
Poll	pool, pond, pit.
Rathad	a road, way.
Réidh	plain, level, smooth.
Riabhach	also as: Riach, drab, greyish, brindled, grizzled.
Righ	king

Roinn   a point, headland, peninsula.
Ros, Ross   a point, promontory.
Roth   wheel of cart, halo.
Ruadh   red, reddish.
Rudha   usually Ru, Rhu, Row, promontory.
Ruighe   also as: Righe, a forearm, cattle run, slope, sheiling.

Sean   old, aged, ancient.
Setr   a sheiling, e.g. Marishader, mare's sheiling. (Norse).
Sgorr, Sgurr, a peak, conical sharp rock, e.g. Sgurr nan Gillean, peak of the
  Scaur   young lads.
Sgreamach   rocky.
Sìth   a fairy. Sìthean, a fairy hillock or knoll.
Sker   skerry, isolated sea rock, e.g. Sulasgeir, pillar skerry.
                   (Norse).
Slettr   smooth, e.g. Slattadale, smooth dale. (Norse).
Slige   a shell, e.g. Sligachan, a shelly place.
Slochd   a deep hollow.
Sneachd   snow.
Socach   snout.
Srath, Strath a wide valley, plain beside a river.
Sròn, Strone   nose, peak, promontory.
Sruth,   a stream, current.
  Struan
Stac   a steep rock, conical hill. (Norse).
Stadr   steading, e.g. Conista, lady's steading; Monkstadt, monk's
                   steading. (Norse).
Stafr   staff, post, e.g. Staffa (*stafr-ey*), pillar isle.(Norse).
Staurr   a stake, pillar. (Norse).
Stob   a point.
Stùc   a pinnacle, peak, conical steep rock.
Suidhe   sitting, resting place.

Tairbeart   also as: Tarbert, Tarbet, an isthmus.
Taigh, Tigh   usually Tay, Ty, a house.
Teallach   a forge.
Tìr, Tyr   country, region, land.
Tobar   a well, spring, fountain.
Toll   a hole.
Tom   a hillock, mound.
Tòrr   a mound, heap, hill.
Tulach   knoll, hillock, eminence. Anglicised forms: Tilly, Tully,
                   Tulloch.

Uachdar   usually Auchter, Ochter, upper land.
Uaine   green.
Uamh   a cave, grave.
Uchd   ascent, face of a hill.
Uig   a nook, bay.
Uisge   water, rain.

Vagr   a bay, e.g. Stornaway (*stjornarvagr*), rudder bay. (Norse).
Vatn   water, lake. Common in Lewis, e.g.Sandwood (*sandabhat*),
                   sandy water or loch. (Norse).

*Map references are given in italic, pictures in **bold** type.*